ROCKS & MINERALS

BACKYARD WORKBOOK

Hands-on Projects, Quizzes, and Activities For Kids

Dan R. Lynch

Acknowledgments

Dan would like to thank his wife, Julie, for her endless support and encouragement during this and all his book projects. Dan would also like to thank his parents, Bob and Nancy, for all their help over the years in obtaining specimens, for their guidance, and for being his best PR people.

Dedication

This book is for all the kids who look at a rock twice before skipping it across the pond.

Disclaimer

This book is meant as an introduction to the practice of rock collecting in general. It does not guarantee your safety when rock collecting in any way—when rock collecting, you do so at your own risk. Neither Adventure Publications nor Dan Lynch is liable for property loss or damage or personal injury that may result from rock collecting. Before you go rock collecting, be sure you have permission to collect on the location, ensure that an adult or adults are present, and always avoid potentially dangerous locations, such as cliffs, areas with moving/deep water, deserts, or areas where wildlife (bears, snakes, cacti, insects) may be a concern. Some rocks and minerals (such as those containing lead) can also be potentially hazardous, so you should always be able to recognize such specimens before you go into the field. (You'll likely need to refer to other field guides or experts to do so.) Finally, be aware that many national, state, and local parks do not allow rock collecting, so again, only collect where you are allowed to do so.

10 9 8 7 6 5 4 3 2

Edited by Brett Ortler
Cover and book design by Fallon Venable
Photo credits on pages 130–131

Rocks & Minerals Backyard Workbook: Hands-on Projects, Quizzes, and Activities For Kids
Copyright © 2021 by Dan R. Lynch
Published by Adventure Publications, an imprint of AdventureKEEN
310 Garfield Street South, Cambridge, Minnesota 55008
(800) 678-7006
www.adventurepublications.net
Printed in China
ISBN 978-1-64755-166-7 (pbk.)

Safety Note

How Kids Can Stay Safe When Rock Collecting

Learning about rocks, minerals, and our amazing planet can be even more fun when you head outside to find your own geological wonders! But whether you are in your backyard or at the beach, you always want to stay safe.

Follow these guidelines:

- Never go out alone! Always bring an adult.

- If you're venturing far, bring a map, a smartphone, or a GPS device so that you don't get lost.

- Always bring water to drink. It's dangerous to be out all day with no water.

- Bring a hat and long clothes to protect you from the sun. You may get hot, but at least you won't get burned.

- Never go into rivers, lakes, or oceans because the water may be deeper or faster than your realize.

- Never go near cliffs! Many are unstable and can fall.

- If a rock that you want is out of reach, just leave it. Your safety is more important than the rock.

- Never go onto private property. (Private property means that someone else owns the land.) If you see signs that say "no trespassing," turn around right away.

- A few rocks can be dangerous to collect. Never taste rocks, and always wash your hands after collecting. If your hands are dirty, don't touch your face or eyes.

Table of Contents

What is Geology?

Rocks and minerals are under your feet every day, but do you know what they are or where they come from?

The study of our planet Earth is called **geology**, and someone who studies geology is a type of scientist called a **geologist**. Not only do geologists find out about how rocks formed, they also learn about how Earth itself formed! Geologists study lots of other things, too, like how the Earth changes over time and which rocks are best to look for when you're trying to find valuable gems or metals in the ground.

Geologists and other scientists study things like **rocks**, **minerals**, **crystals**, **fossils**, and **landforms**. All of these things are important for understanding the history of Earth.

Emerald

Diamond

But if you don't know what some of those things are, that's OK because we'll learn about them in this book.

Geology studies all things about the Earth beneath your feet, from common rocks to amazing landforms, like the colorful hills below, and how they came to be.

When we look at rocks, we can also find and study incredible fossils of ancient life, or even valuable gems.

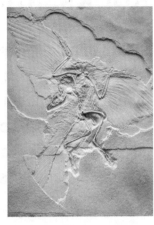

Archaeopteryx fossil

What are Minerals, Crystals, Rocks, and Fossils?

1. Minerals: *Minerals are special chemicals that usually form in the ground inside rocks.* When minerals harden, they form crystals. There are many different kinds of minerals. Some are shiny and some are dull, and some are very colorful but others are not. Minerals can form in many different ways.

A blocky pyrite crystal

2. Crystals: *Crystals are hardened minerals.* Each mineral forms crystals of a specific shape. For example, the mineral called pyrite usually grows crystals shaped like square blocks. And no matter where in the world you find pyrite, chances are it'll have the same blocky shape.

There are many kinds of crystal shapes, such as sharp points, flat plates, and some that even look like little trees!

Two common kinds of rocks: granite (top) and basalt (bottom)

3. Rocks: *Rocks are hard materials made up of a mixture of minerals.* The minerals are tightly packed together. And each different kind of rock contains a different mixture of minerals in it. This makes different kinds of rocks look very different from each other. It's kind of like having different types of cookies—a chocolate chip cookie and an oatmeal cookie are both cookies, but they have totally different ingredients.

A group of quartz crystals

Rocks can form either deep inside the Earth or on the Earth's surface where we can see them. Rocks come in all kinds of colors, and some have layers or stripes, and others have lots of spots. When you see a speckled rock, look carefully at each different colored spot—those are all different minerals.

This is a fossil leaf preserved in the surface of a rock.

4. Fossils: *Fossils are special kinds of rocks that contain traces of ancient plants and animals.* Things like animal teeth, bones, and plant leaves can be preserved in certain rocks. We can learn a lot about plants and animals that lived a long time ago by comparing fossils to animals that are alive today. Many fossils are millions of years old!

Matching: Crystal, Rock, or Fossil?

Using what you've learned about minerals, crystals, rocks, and fossils, draw a line from each photo to the label that you think best describes it.

The most important things to remember:

1. Minerals are natural chemicals in the Earth that have hardened.

2. Hardened minerals make special shapes called crystals.

3. Rocks are hard materials made up of a mixture of minerals all jumbled together.

1. Rhyolite

2. Magnetite

3. Granite

4. Wulfenite

5. *Knightia*

6. Scallop

Rock   **Crystal**   **Fossil**

Answers on page 119! ☞

Our Planet Earth

The Earth beneath your feet may seem solid, but it's always changing! Even mountains and oceans will some day be gone and replaced by something else. That's because deep inside the Earth it is very hot—so hot that even solid rocks can melt! All of that heat makes the inside of the Earth move around very slowly.

The Earth has five main layers. They are:

1. The Crust: The outside of the Earth is called the crust. The crust is where all plants and animals live—including you. It is made up of hard rocks, like the ones that you can pick up outside.

2. The Upper Mantle: The next layer down is called the upper mantle. It is heated by the layers below it and is very hot. When rocks from the crust are pushed down into the Earth, they melt in the upper mantle. The molten rocks here are called **magma**. The magma in the upper mantle moves and flows very slowly, a little bit like syrup!

3. The Lower Mantle: Below the upper mantle is the lower mantle, where it is even hotter. But the rocks there are buried so deep (and there's so much pressure) that they can't melt, so the lower mantle is solid.

4. The Outer Core: The outer core is near the center of the planet. It is so hot that all the rocks there are melted and soft.

5. The Inner Core: At the very center of the Earth is the inner core, which is a big ball made almost entirely of metal! Specifically, it is composed mostly of iron and nickel. Even though it is very hot, the metals here don't melt, and the inner core is solid.

Labeling: Earth's Layers

We live on the thin outside of the Earth. All of the mountains and oceans are part of it. This layer is called the:

1. _____

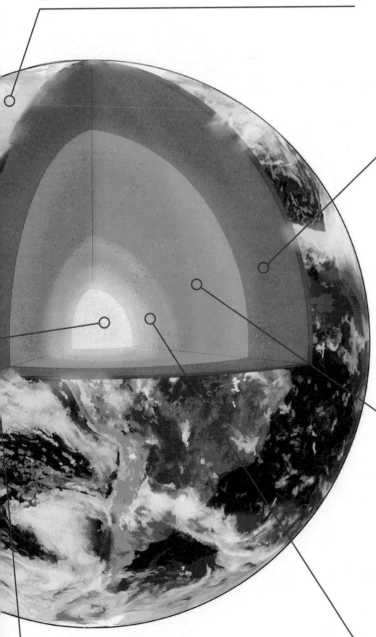

The next layer down is hot and soft because it is made up of melted rocks. It is always flowing and moving. This layer is called the:

2. _____

Even though this layer is also very hot, the rocks there don't melt because they are buried so deep down. This layer is called the:

3. _____

This layer is near the center of the Earth. There it is so hot that everything melts. The melted rocks here flow and swirl around. This layer is called the:

4. _____

The very hot ball of solid metal at the center of the Earth is called the:

5. _____

Answers on page 119! ☞

The Earth's Crust

We live on top of the Earth's thin crust. The crust is hard and made of different kinds of rocks. But the crust is not just one solid piece. Instead, the Earth's crust is made up of many separate pieces called **tectonic plates**. The tectonic plates fit together like huge puzzle pieces. But they're always moving slowly because of the hot melted rocks flowing below them in the upper mantle.

When tectonic plates move, some move away from each other, others crash into each other, and some plates can slide past each other.

These different kinds of movements can form valleys, mountains, and oceans, as well as cause earthquakes and volcanic eruptions.

Earth's Tectonic Plates

This map shows the locations of Earth's tectonic plates. Each of these plates is a huge sheet of rock that moves slowly. Notice how the continents usually sit on one plate, but the oceans sit upon several plates.

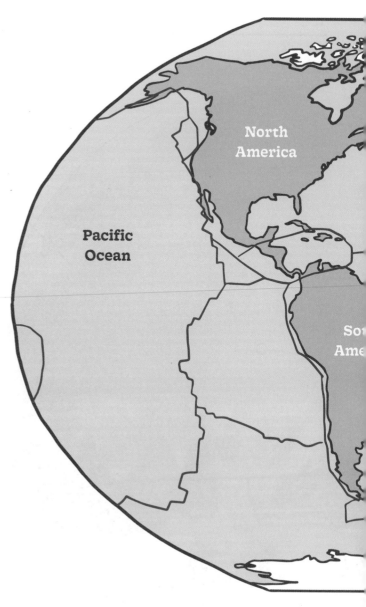

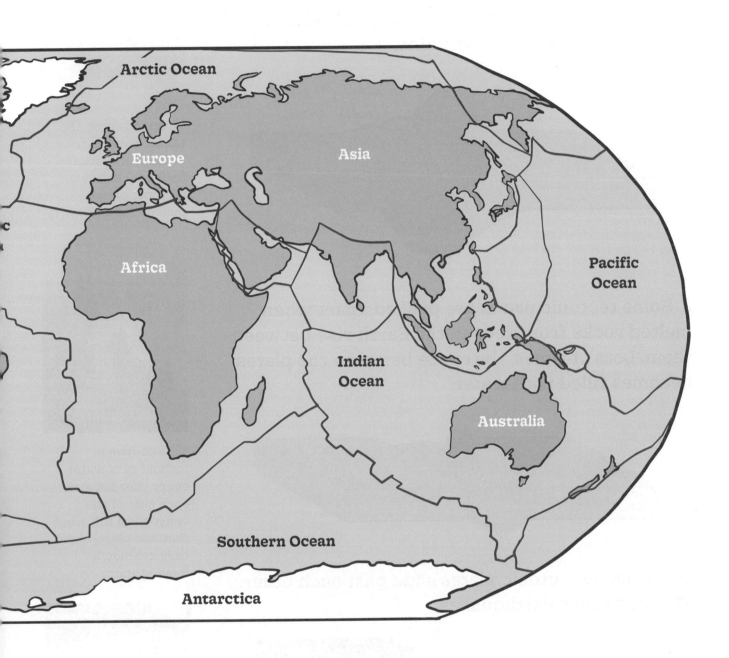

Arctic Ocean

Europe

Asia

Africa

Pacific
Ocean

Indian
Ocean

Australia

Southern Ocean

Antarctica

Tectonic Plate Movement

Here are a few of the ways tectonic plates move:

1. When tectonic plates push into each other, one is often pushed down into the Earth while the other is pushed up to form mountains.

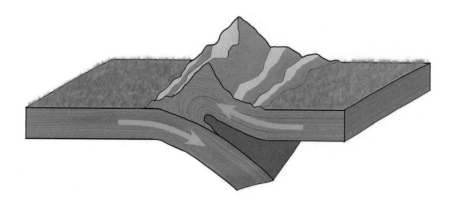

Mount Everest, the tallest mountain in the world, was formed when two tectonic plates pushed rock upward.

2. Some tectonic plates are pushed apart when melted rocks from deep in the Earth rise between them. Lots of times, the space between the plates becomes filled with water.

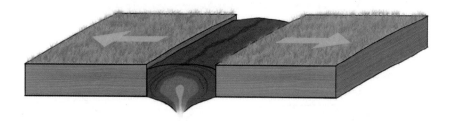

This canyon in Iceland gets wider every year because each side of the canyon is a different tectonic plate, and they are slowly moving apart.

3. And some tectonic plates slide past each other. This can cause earthquakes.

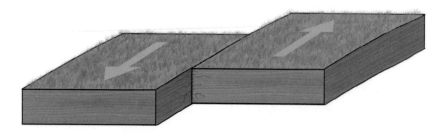

When two tectonic plates slide past each other, it can cause earthquakes that can cause major disasters.

Activity: Make Your Own Tectonic Plates

Using flat pieces of clay, try to recreate these tectonic plate motions. For example, see what happens when you push two sheets of modeling clay together. One of them might rise up to make a hill or mountain! Experiment with differently shaped pieces of clay, or try making one sheet thicker than the other.

1. These two pieces of clay can act like tectonic plates. See how one is much thinner than the other? This represents the different kinds of tectonic plates.

Hint: If your clay is too sticky to easily slide along a table, try putting a little piece of paper towel under each piece to help it slide more easily.

2. When pushed together, the top of the thicker one starts to roll over the thinner one, while the thinner one starts to push underneath.

3. Keep pushing them together and the thicker one may rise up into a shape that looks like a hill or mountain—a lot like how tectonic plates form mountains.

Timeline of Earth's History

The Earth is very old—around 4.6 billion years old!—and lots of different plants and animals have lived on our planet throughout that time. Some that appeared long ago are still around today, like fish, but others went extinct (died out), like the dinosaurs. At first, there was no life that lived on dry land—not even plants! All life on Earth began in the oceans and slowly moved onto land over millions of years.

Scientists organize the Earth's lifetime into chunks called periods. Each period saw different kinds of life appearing and disappearing. Let's look at the timeline of Earth and when different plants and animals first appeared.

After studying the timeline, answer these questions:

1. Trilobites first appeared in the Cambrian Period, around 521 million years ago. But they went extinct 252 million years later at the end of another period. Which period was their last?

_____

2. Stromatolites are rounded structures made by what kinds of organisms?

_____

Formation of the *Earth* 4.6 billion years ago.

Answers on page 119! ☞

Trilobites were sea creatures that lived in the oceans. They were around for a long time. They lived from 521 million years ago to 252 million years ago, but they are extinct now.

The **first fish** started to appear in the oceans around 530 million years ago. The very earliest fish were different from most fish we know now—they didn't have jaws, just like lamprey (a weird, eel-like sort of fish) today.

Precambrian Period
Began: 4.6 billion years ago
Ended: 541 million years ago

Cambrian Period
Began: 541 million years ago
Ended: 485 million years ago

One of the earliest kinds of life on earth was tiny bacteria. Cyanobacteria, also called blue-green algae, has been living in the oceans for about 3.6 billion years (and maybe earlier), and are still around today! These bacteria live grouped together in round, mushroom-shaped rocky structures called **stromatolites**.

Mollusks first appeared in the oceans around the beginning of the Cambrian Period, 541 million years ago. Mollusks are soft, boneless animals that often have a shell. Clams, snails, and octopuses are mollusks.

Timeline of Earth's History

They may look like ocean plants, but **crinoids** are animals. They appeared 480 million years ago and are still around today.

Sharks first appeared in the oceans around 425 million years ago.

Ordovician Period
Began: 485 million years ago
Ended: 443 million years ago

Silurian Period
Began: 443 million years ago
Ended: 419 million years ago

This strange fossil is from a group of animals known as Orthoceras. They were squid-like animals with a long shell and lived around 470 to 442 million years ago.

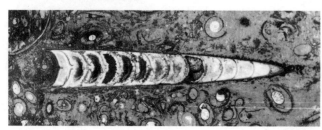

The **first animals appeared on land** around 419 million years ago at the end of the Silurian Period—they were tiny animals with no backbones, and were a lot like millipedes and spiders we have today.

Ferns were some of the first leafy land plants and appeared around 380 million years ago.

Conifer trees (trees with seed cones) appeared around 310 million years ago.

Quiz Time

After studying the timeline, answer these questions:

1. When did the first fish appear?

_____

2. The first animals with backbones that lived only on dry land appeared in what period?

_____

3. What were the first animals with backbones to walk on land?

_____

Devonian Period
Began: 419 million years ago
Ended: 359 million years ago

Carboniferous Period
Began: 359 million years ago
Ended: 299 million years ago

Some of the first animals with backbones to walk on land were **amphibians**, around 370 million years ago. They were major predators back then. They lived mostly in the water but could come on land.

Reptiles, like lizards, appeared 312 million years ago. They were the first animals with backbones that only lived on land and not partially in the water.

Answers on page 119! ☞

Timeline of Earth's History

Giant insects, such as giant relatives of dragonflies called *Meganeura* (which had a wingspan over two feet!), lived around 305 million years ago.

Around 275 million years ago, a group of animals called **therapsids** appeared. They were a little bit like half-reptile, half-mammal animals! They are the distant relatives of all mammals.

Carboniferous Period

Permian Period
Began: 299 million years ago
Ended: 252 million years ago

Quiz Time

After studying the timeline, answer these questions:

1. Both dinosaurs and mammals appeared during which period?

_____

2. Mammals became the dominant species in the Paleogene Period, after the dinosaurs went extinct. Without the dinosaurs around to eat them, what happened to many kinds of mammals?

_____

Dimetrodon were animals that lived during the Permian Period. They may have looked like dinosaurs, but they were actually more closely related to mammals than to reptiles.

Answers on page 119! ☞

Not long after dinosaurs appeared, so did mammals! The **first furry, warm-blooded mammals** were very small so that they could hide from predators, like dinosaurs. They appeared around 220 million years ago.

Some of the biggest dinosaurs started to appear in the Jurassic Period. *Brontosaurus* first appeared around 156 million years ago and lived until about 147 million years ago.

Triassic Period
Began: 252 million years ago
Ended: 201 million years ago

Jurassic Period
Began: 201 million years ago
Ended: 145 million years ago

The first dinosaurs were small, like this *Coelophysis (say it "see-lo-fy-sis")*. Dinosaurs began to appear around 233 million years ago.

Many of the strangest dinosaurs began to appear in the Jurassic too. *Stegosaurus*, with their spiked tails, lived from about 155 to 150 million years ago.

Timeline of Earth's History

The **first birds** began to appear around 121 million years ago. Back then, they had teeth! All birds evolved from dinosaurs, which means that all birds today are directly related to dinosaurs, like *Tyrannosaurus rex!*

Dinosaurs went extinct 66 million years ago.

The first **primates**, like monkeys, appeared around 55 million years ago. Primates are very smart and are the distant relatives of humans like you and me!

Cretaceous Period
Began: 145 million years ago
Ended: 66 million years ago

Paleogene Period
Began: 66 million years ago
Ended: 23 million years ago

The mighty *Tyrannosaurus rex* and stout *Triceratops* appeared around the same time, 68 million years ago. *Tyrannosaurus rex* likely hunted the *Triceratops*.

After the dinosaurs went extinct, **mammals** could grow to much bigger sizes, like this giant ground sloth that lived around 35 million years ago. Some ground sloths were nearly 20 feet long!

The largest shark ever, the *megalodon*, was as big as a bus! It ate whales and appeared about 23 million years ago, surviving until about 3.6 million years ago.

Saber-toothed cats were large and had enormous fangs; they lived from around 2.5 million years ago to as recently as 10,000 years ago.

Quiz Time

After studying the timeline, answer these questions:

1. What animals are still alive today that are directly related to dinosaurs?

_____

2. Dinosaurs lived in three time periods. Which periods were they?

_____

3. Did *T. rex* ever fight a *Stegosaurus?*

_____

Neogene Period
Began: 23 million years ago
Ended: 2.6 million years ago

Quaternary Period
Began: 2.6 million years ago
Still continues today.

Today, you're reading this book! ☞

Mastodons were large muscular animals like elephants. They first appeared 5 million years ago and lived until about 10,000 years ago.

We are a very young species. **Humans** appeared around 300,000 years ago.

Answers on page 119! ☞

Rock Layers

The Earth's crust has lots of rocks in it that we can find and study. Some rocks are much older than others and formed a very long time ago. But how do we know which rocks are older?

One way that we can learn about the age of rocks is by looking at **rock strata**. Strata is a scientific word that means "layers," so when we study rock strata, what we're studying are the layers of rock that make up the Earth's crust. It's like looking at the different layers in a fancy cake.

The most important thing to know about rock layers is that younger layers form on top of older layers. Each layer can be a completely different kind of rock, but the oldest ones are at the bottom.

Activity: Create Your Own Layers

What you'll need:

- A clear jar or bowl
- Different-colored sand, gravel, and/or dirt

1. Put some dirt or sand in a clear container so that it forms a layer that covers the bottom. Then, take a different color of sand or a different kind of dirt and make another layer above the bottom layer. Keep repeating this with different sand or dirt until the jar is filled. Then take a look at the layers you made.

2. The layers you made are a lot like rock layers. Since you put the bottom layer in the jar first, it is older than the top layer, which you put in last. And if some of your layers weren't perfectly flat, look how they affected the shape of the layers above them.

3. Try this activity again and place some small toys or stones in the various layers to represent fossils!

Quiz Time

Answer these questions using the image on the left:

1. Which layer is the oldest?

_____

2. Do you think that the *T. rex* and the *Triceratops* (shown in the fossils in the rocks at left) lived at the same time?

_____

3. Which is older: the *T. rex* fossil or the *Triceratops* fossil?

_____

Answers on page 119! ☞

Weathering

Rocks may seem so solid that nothing could hurt them, but all it takes is some water! When water, like rain and waves, hits a rock for many years, it can wash away little pieces of the rock and change its shape. This can even happen to huge rock layers! Other things like wind, ice, and even plants can also change and break rocks. This is called **weathering**, and it is a powerful force that shapes the Earth's crust.

Here are some of the different ways that weathering can change rocks.

When **water** hits rock over and over, it slowly washes away tiny pieces of it. Over many years, this can eventually wear away the whole rock. This huge hole in the cliff was made by **waves.**

Wind can blow around little pieces of sand, and when that sand hits a rock, it can chip tiny pieces off of it. These huge rock arches were carved by the wind blowing sand against the rock for many years.

When water freezes to become **ice**, it expands, which means it gets bigger. If a crack in a rock has some water in it and then the water gets cold enough to freeze, the expanding ice can split the rock! These cracks were made by ice.

Glaciers are enormous sheets of ice that flow very slowly, like a river of ice. They are very heavy and can crush rocks beneath them. This glacier is carving a whole valley into these mountains.

Sometimes natural **acids** in the ground can **dissolve** soft rocks. This means that the rocks are slowly absorbed into water. This can happen underground, which makes sinkholes open up, like this one.

Plants may seem weaker than rocks, but when their roots get into the cracks in rocks and grow bigger, they can split the rock. Cliffs can form when plants break up the rocks and make them fall.

Landforms

The rocks and rock layers in Earth's crust take all kinds of shapes! These are called landforms, and they include things like mountains and valleys. Some landforms are formed by the moving tectonic plates and others are formed when wind, water, and ice shape and carve rocks (that's called weathering). Read more about landforms on pages 92–105.

Rivers are paths that water makes as it flows downhill. Rivers wash away rocks and are a form of weathering.

Oceans are huge bodies of water that form when two tectonic plates spread apart and water fills in between them.

Lakes are bodies of water that form in low spots made by weathering, like rain and ice.

Deserts are very dry areas that don't get much rain, sometimes because nearby mountains stop the rain clouds from getting there.

Tall **mountains** can form a few different ways, but they usually form when tectonic plates crash into each other and one is pushed upward! Young mountains are sharp and jagged, but older mountains are lower and more rounded from weathering.

Volcanoes are places where melted rock is pushed out of the Earth and onto the surface. These are often the result of tectonic plate movements.

Plateaus *(say it "plah-tohs")* are like hills with flat tops. They can form by tectonic plate movements or by weathering or often by both.

Valleys are low areas between mountains. They can be formed by tectonic plate movements or by weathering or often by both.

Canyons are like a deep valley with steep sides. They were formed by weathering, when rivers washed away the rock.

Quiz Time: Name the Landform

Using what you've learned about different landforms, answer these questions:

1. Which landform from this list is usually formed by the movement of tectonic plates?

A. Canyon

B. Mountain

C. River

2. Which landform from this list is usually formed by weathering?

A. Volcano

B. Ocean

C. Canyon

3. Which of these mountain ranges is oldest?

A.

B.

4. Which landform blocks rain clouds from getting to deserts?

A. Mountain

B. Plateau

C. Lake

5. Which of these landforms can form by both tectonic plate movements and by weathering?

A. Valleys

B. Volcanoes

C. Plateaus

6. Which of these landforms is formed when tectonic plates spread apart?

A. Mountain

B. River

C. Ocean

Answers on page 119! ☞

Minerals

Minerals from when special chemicals in or on the Earth come together and harden to form crystals. There are thousands of different minerals. Each mineral has a specific set of "ingredients" that doesn't change, no matter where in the world you find it. These ingredients are called **elements**, which can be thought of as "building blocks" that make up everything, including minerals!

For example, table salt is actually a mineral called halite. The "ingredients" that make up halite are the elements sodium and chlorine. No matter where in the world you find halite, it is always formed from the same combination of sodium and chlorine.

The most exciting thing about minerals is their crystals! **Crystals** are the shapes minerals take when they harden. They form when a mineral is pure and has enough room to grow. Each mineral forms crystals of a specific shape.

For example, halite forms as cubes, sometimes in groups that are stuck together. No matter where in the world you find halite, it will form as cube crystals. If you look at table salt under a magnifying glass, you might even see some cube crystals there too.

There are lots of different possible crystal shapes. From blocky shapes to pointy shapes, or flat shapes to lumpy shapes.

Naturally formed halite crystals, also known as table salt

A nice cube-shaped crystal of halite

With a magnifying glass or microscope, you may find cube-shaped halite crystals in common table salt!

Matching: Crystals

Different minerals can have different crystal shapes, and there are a lot of them! Get to know a few of the common shapes and appearances of minerals by matching these mineral photos to the label that best describes them.

1. Feldspar

2. Mica

3. Quartz

4. Garnet

5. Pyrite

6. Beryl

7. Hematite

8. Copper

A. Barrel-Shaped: Some minerals form crystals that are short with flat ends.

B. Ball-Shaped: Some minerals form crystals that look a bit like a soccer ball.

C. Pointy: Some minerals can form crystals that have sharp tips.

D. Cube-Shaped: Some minerals form crystals shaped like perfect cubes.

E. Grape-Like: Many minerals form lumpy masses that look a bit like bunches of grapes.

F. Blocky: Many minerals form crystals that are big and blocky with no sharp tips, but they are not perfect cubes, either.

G. Tree-Like: Some minerals can form complex crystals that branch out like a tree.

H. Flaky: Lots of minerals form thin, flaky crystals that grow together in layers.

Answers on page 119! ☞

Minerals

Minerals can form in many different ways. In fact, some geologists specialize in studying the different ways minerals can form—they're called **mineralogists**. Just one of the many ways nice crystals form is when hot water from deep inside the Earth rises up into the holes inside hard rocks. The hot water has lots of minerals dissolved in it. That means that it has lots of tiny particles of minerals in the water. When the water begins to cool, it leaves those particles behind inside the spaces in rocks. Eventually, those particles can combine to form minerals and crystals.

Most minerals form inside rocks, usually inside a space or hole where they can grow. Sometimes they can fill the space completely, and other times they may only form a crust around the inside of the hole.

Activity: Dissolving Minerals

With an adult's help, you can test how minerals dissolve in warm water. Heat a small amount of water in a cup, and then add some table salt (halite) to it and stir it. Eventually, the salt will dissolve, or disappear into the water—now the water has a mineral in it! If you leave the cup alone for a few days and let the water dry up, then you'll see that the salt was left behind as a crust of tiny crystals on the bottom of the cup. This is similar to how hot water in the Earth moves minerals around and the way that crystals grow inside the holes in rocks as the water dries up.

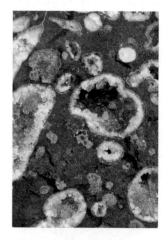

This photo shows holes in a rock that were partially filled with little quartz crystals.

This illustration shows us how hot water from deep in the Earth can rise up into a hole in a rock and leave crystals behind.

Matching: Luster

Minerals and their crystals not only have different shapes and colors, but they also have different lusters. **Luster** is how shiny a mineral is. Some minerals, like diamonds, are very lustrous, or shiny, but others are very dull and not shiny at all.

We describe luster by comparing it to another material. For example, a mineral that has a "glassy luster" is shiny like glass.

Here are some common lusters—match the labels to the mineral photo that shows that kind of luster.

1. Feldspar
(say it "feld-spar")

2. Chalcopyrite
(say it "kal-co-pie-rite")

3. Jasper
(say it "jass-per")

4. Quartz
(say it "kwarts")

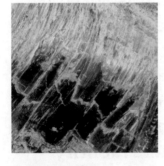

5. Serpentine
(say it "ser-pen-teen")

6. Limonite
(say it "lime-oh-nite")

A. Metallic: Luster that is shiny and reflective like metal.

B. Waxy: Luster that is a little shiny, like wax.

C. Glassy: Very shiny luster that resembles glass.

D. Greasy: This luster is fairly shiny, a little bit like wet hair.

E. Dull: Minerals with dull luster aren't very shiny at all.

F. Earthy: Minerals that are not shiny and instead often look gritty like dirt.

Answers on page 119! ☞

Mineral Hardness

Every mineral has a specific hardness that we can test with tools. *Hardness* tells you how easy it is to scratch a mineral. Some minerals are so soft that you can scratch them with just your fingernails, while others are so hard that almost nothing will scratch them. Finding out how hard a mineral is can help you identify it.

Mineral hardness is described with the **Mohs Hardness Scale,** which measures mineral hardness on a scale of 1 to 10. A mineral with a hardness of 1 is very soft, and 10 is very hard. Most minerals are somewhere in the middle, usually between 3 and 7. You can test the hardness of a mineral by scratching it with a tool that you already know the hardness of. The chart on pages 38 shows you the hardness of some common minerals as well as some common tools used to test them.

For example, if you have a mineral that is scratched by a U.S. nickel coin, which is a 3.5 hardness, then you know it is softer than 3.5 on the scale. But if your fingernail, which is a hardness of 2.5, won't scratch it, then you know it is harder than 2.5. This would make the mineral a 3 in hardness. Then you can use that hardness to help identify the mineral you've found by looking up minerals with a hardness of 3.

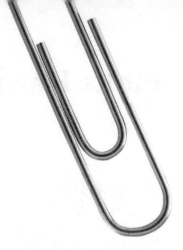

This paperclip is made of steel.

Activity: Hardness Test

Once you've found some minerals, you can test their hardness to try to figure out what they are! With an adult's help, you can use the tools on the chart on the next page to try scratching your mineral. Tools that are too soft won't leave a mark on the mineral. But tools that are harder than the mineral will leave a mark, so be sure to make only a small scratch on the backside of the mineral.

You can buy hardness test kits that have a tool of each hardness, but you can also find your own hardness test tools.

You could also see what other things might scratch a mineral. Copper coins, paperclips, or even a piece of plastic might scratch a mineral.

Give it a try: Plastic is softer than metal, so see if a plastic toy can scratch your mineral. If not, then try a coin or a paperclip. If those scratch it, then you know the mineral is harder than plastic but softer than those metal objects.

A U.S. penny coin: ones with a date before 1982 are copper; those produced after 1982 are mostly made of zinc.

This U.S. nickel coin is made from copper and nickel.

These toy blocks are made from plastic.

Mohs Hardness Scale

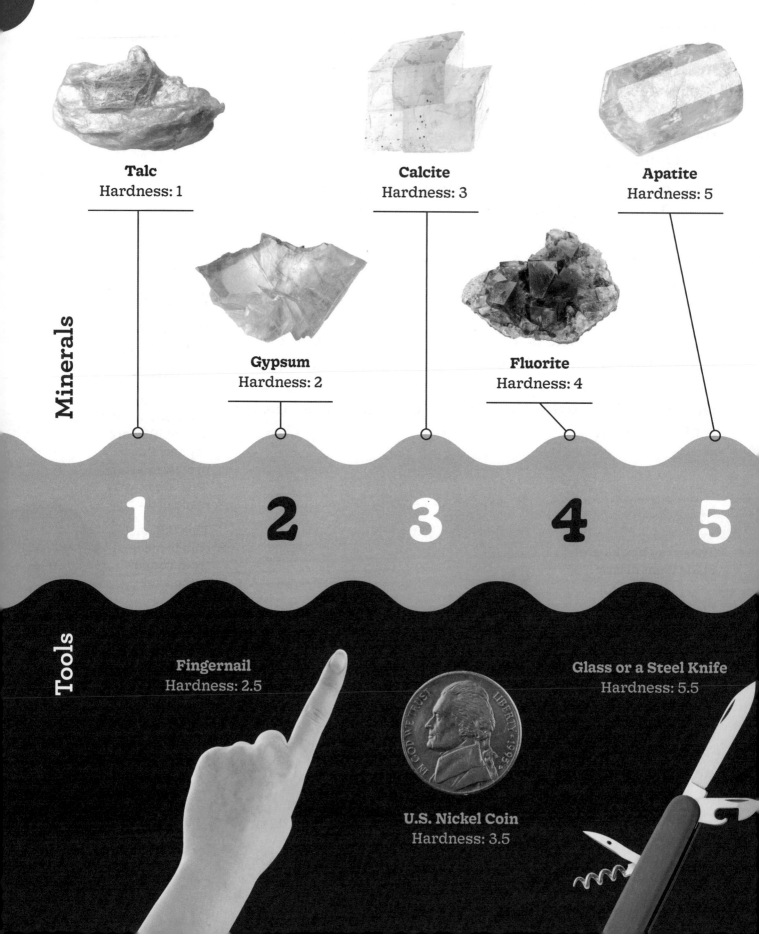

Minerals

Talc
Hardness: 1

Gypsum
Hardness: 2

Calcite
Hardness: 3

Fluorite
Hardness: 4

Apatite
Hardness: 5

1   2   3   4   5

Tools

Fingernail
Hardness: 2.5

Glass or a Steel Knife
Hardness: 5.5

U.S. Nickel Coin
Hardness: 3.5

Quartz
Hardness: 7

Corundum
Hardness: 9

Orthoclase Feldspar
Hardness: 6

Topaz
Hardness: 8

Diamond
Hardness: 10

6   7   8   9   10

**Unglazed Porcelain
or Streak Plate**
Hardness: 6.5

Hardened Steel File
Hardness: 7.5

Silicon Carbide Drill Bit
Hardness: 9.5

Mineral Colors

Minerals can be found in almost any color, and sometimes one mineral can be found in many different colors, depending on where it formed. For example, the mineral called beryl can be gray, green, blue, yellow, red, and more, all depending on what kind of rock it formed inside of. We have different names for each kind of colored beryl, but they're all the same mineral!

Beryl is often gray or brown.

Blue beryl is called aquamarine.

Green beryl is called emerald.

Yellow beryl is called heliodor.

Red beryl is called bixbite.

Not all minerals are so colorful. Many are clear and have no color at all, and many more are just white or gray. Sometimes a white mineral can be colored differently by other minerals that have stained it, but its true color is white.

Pure quartz crystals are usually white or clear.

Sometimes iron minerals will stain quartz, making it look red.

Labeling: Colored Quartz

Quartz is a very common mineral that is usually clear or white. But sometimes it can form somewhere that gives it more color, such as these examples that have special names:

- Pink quartz is called **rose quartz.**
- Gray or brown quartz is called **smoky quartz.**
- Purple quartz is called **amethyst.**
- Yellow quartz is called **citrine.**
- Totally black quartz is called **morion quartz.**

Based on these descriptions, label each of the quartz photos below:

1. _____

   _____

2. _____

   _____

3. _____

   _____

4. _____

   _____

5. _____

   _____

Answers on page 119! ☞

Streak Color

Since some minerals, like beryl, can be found in many different colors, color is not a very good trait to use to identify some minerals. But the color of a mineral can seem to change when it has been crushed into a powder. For example, beryl always makes a white powder when crushed, no matter what color the crystal was.

Rub a mineral on a streak plate to find its streak color.

But you don't have to crush a whole specimen to see what color its powder is. Instead, you can scratch it on a special piece of tile called a "streak plate." When you scratch a mineral on this plate, it leaves behind a powdered **streak** of color.

Next time you find a mineral, test it with a streak plate to see what color its powder is. Along with its hardness and crystal shape, its streak color can be very useful for figuring out what you found!

Note: If you can't find a streak plate to buy, have an adult help you find an unglazed piece of porcelain, such as the back side of a bathroom tile—it will work the same!

Different Colored Streaks

Some minerals, especially metallic minerals, can have a streak color that is very different from their crystal color. Marcasite, for example, is a brassy yellow mineral that has a gray streak color.

Matching: Streaks

Sometimes it can be tricky to guess a mineral's streak color, but here are a few tips that might help.

Some metallic minerals (but not all) have streak colors that are very different from their color when whole. This can make them hard to guess, but sometimes you can see a hint of those colors on the mineral even before you check their streak color. Glassy minerals often have a white streak, no matter what color their crystals are. Some soft minerals can have a pale streak color that resembles their crystal colors.

Using what you learned about hardness and streak, try to guess which streak colors on the right belong to the minerals below. Don't worry if you get some wrong—guessing streak color can be hard until you've learned a lot about minerals.

1. Hematite is a metallic mineral with a hardness of 5 to 6.

2. Goethite is a metallic mineral with a hardness of 5 to 5.5.

3. Chlorite is a mineral with a hardness of 2 to 2.5.

4. Garnet is a glassy mineral with a hardness of 6.5 to 7.5.

5. Chrysocolla is a mineral with a hardness of 2 to 4.

6. Pyrite is a metallic mineral with a hardness of 6 to 6.5.

 A.   B.

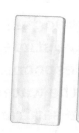 C.   D.

  E.   F.

Answers on page 119! ☞

43

Activity: Grow Your Own Crystals

To better understand how crystals can form, you can grow your own at home! You'll need an adult's help, but it's easy to do.

What you'll need:

- Alum in granular form, about 1.5 cups
- Water, 1.5 cups
- A 32-ounce wide-mouth canning jar
- A small saucepan
- A stirring utensil (something disposable, like a wooden stir stick, is preferable)
- A piece of string at least 5 inches long
- A pencil, dowel, or other short stick-like object

Note: Parents, there are several types of alum available. For the best results, look for alum consisting of potassium aluminum sulfate—it should specify on the label. This may not be the kind you find in the spice aisle of a grocery store.

1. Boil 1.5 cups of water in a small sauce pan.

2. Begin to add the alum one tablespoon at a time, stirring as you add it. The alum will dissolve in the boiling water.

3. Keep adding alum until you have stirred in about 22 tablespoons. By this point, the water should be over-saturated with alum and you should see some grains in the water that won't dissolve. This is called super saturation, and it will ensure that crystals can grow quickly.

Warning: This activity can stain pans and dishes, so only use older or inexpensive utensils!

4. Carefully pour the hot, super-saturated water into the jar.

5. Tie the string to the pencil or other stick-like object, and place the stick across the top of the jar. Center the string so it is suspended without touching the sides or the bottom of the jar.

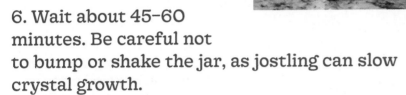

6. Wait about 45–60 minutes. Be careful not to bump or shake the jar, as jostling can slow crystal growth.

7. After 45–60 minutes, lift the string to see what crystals have grown! You may have one large crystal or several smaller ones. The longer you leave the string in the water, the larger the crystals will grow. However, if you leave them too long, they may grow so large that they fill the bottom of the jar and you'll be unable to get them out.

Note: In this example, two crystals have grown on the string. The larger one is about one inch wide.

You just grew crystals from hot, mineral-rich water, just like the way many grow in nature!

Activity: Crystal Seeds

When crystals grow, they build upon themselves by attracting more of the mineral. It's like when you roll a snowball around in the snow to make it bigger—the snow clings to more snow. It's the same with minerals, and you can test this by taking one of the crystals you grew and using it to grow an even bigger crystal. This is called "crystal seeding" because a small crystal (the "seed") is used to make a bigger one.

In this example, we carefully cut off the smaller bottom crystal on the string shown on the previous page, and just used the larger crystal at the top, leaving it attached to the string.

What you'll need:

- Alum in granular form, about 1.5 cups
- Water, 1.5 cups
- A 32-ounce wide-mouth canning jar
- A small saucepan
- A stirring utensil (something disposable, like a wooden stir stick, is preferable)
- A small alum crystal pre-grown on a string
- A pencil, dowel, or other short stick-like object

Note: Parents, there are several types of alum available. For the best results, look for alum consisting of potassium aluminum sulfate—it should specify on the label. This may not be the kind you find in the spice aisle of a grocery store.

1. Boil another batch of water super-saturated with alum, but instead of pouring it into a jar right away, take it off the stove top and let the pan of water cool for 10–15 minutes first.

2. Pour the slightly cooled water into a clean, dry jar.

Warning: This activity can stain pans and dishes, so only use older or inexpensive utensils!

3. Using a pencil or stick, as before, suspend the seed crystal into the water, being careful to not let it touch the sides or the bottom of the jar.

4. Wait 15-30 minutes, then carefully lift the string to check on your crystal. Is it getting bigger?

5. Keep carefully checking your crystal every 10 minutes or so until it is of large size. But don't wait too long, because it could grow so large that it touches the bottom of the jar, which will prevent it from growing sharp crystal shapes.

Note: See how big this crystal got? It now measures about three inches, about triple the size it started from!

You can get all kinds of different results by using more or less alum, letting the water cool longer before putting in the string, or even by putting other objects in the water for the crystals to grow upon. Experiment for different results!

What's Going on in the Jar?

To understand how these crystals formed in the jar, let's look at the science happening. Alum powder, as well as other things, like salt or sugar, will dissolve in cold water, but only a little bit. Cold water won't hold very much dissolved alum in it. But if you heat up the water, a lot more will dissolve in it. And as long as the water stays very hot, that alum will stay dissolved in it. But when the water starts to cool down, it can no longer hold the dissolved alum, which begins to clump together and harden. This is called **precipitation**. As it precipitates and hardens, it starts to crystallize into the cool shapes you see in the jar.

Minerals can form in many different ways, but lots of them form by precipitation. In the super-salty Dead Sea, salt crystals precipitate right onto the rocks on the shore.

Salt crystals along the shore of the Dead Sea

Common Minerals

There are thousands of minerals around the world, but only a few are considered common. Let's take a look at some of the ones you're most likely to find or buy in shops. You can use the checkbox next to each mineral to check off ones you already have in your collection.

☐ **Quartz** *(say it "kwartz")*
Hardness: 7

Quartz is the most common mineral in the Earth's crust! It is usually glassy and can form in clear, pointed crystals. It is very common as rounded pebbles on beaches.

☐ **Jasper**
Hardness: 7

Jasper is actually a special kind of quartz. It is opaque (light can't shine through it) and has a waxy luster. It can be found in almost any color, and it is very common in rivers.

☐ **Chalcedony** *(say it "kal-seh-duh-nee")*
Hardness: 7

Chalcedony is another special kind of quartz. It is translucent (it will let some light pass through it) and has a waxy luster. It can be found in many different colors and is common in rivers.

☐ **Opal**
Hardness: 5.5–6.5

Opal is very glassy and brittle. It does not form crystals but fills in spaces in rocks. It is usually white but can be found in other colors too. It is mostly found in desert regions.

Pyrite *(say it "pie-rite")*
Hardness: 6–6.5

Pyrite is a yellowish metallic mineral that can be very shiny. Because of its color, it is also called "fool's gold." But pyrite is much more common. Its crystals can form perfect cubes, like blocks.

Hematite *(say it "hee-muh-tite")*
Hardness: 5–6

Hematite is a very common mineral. It contains iron, and we mine it to make steel. It is black and metallic, but it can turn a rusty red color too. It can form lumpy masses or crystals shaped like blades.

Goethite *(say it "ger-tite")*
Hardness: 5–5.5

Goethite is a very common mineral that has iron in it. It is black and metallic, but it can also turn to a rusty yellowish color. You've probably already seen goethite; any time you see a rusty spot on a rock or metal, it's probably goethite!

Magnetite *(say it "mag-nuh-tite")*
Hardness: 5.5–6.5

Magnetite is a common mineral that is usually black and metallic. It has iron in it, and it is special because it is magnetic. This means a magnet will stick to it. You can easily find magnetite on the beach by putting a magnet in the sand—anything that sticks is probably magnetite!

Common Minerals

☐ **Feldspar** *(say it "feld-spar")*
Hardness: 6–6.5

Feldspar may not look exciting, but it's one of the most important minerals! It is very common and is found in most kinds of rocks. We call it a "rock builder" because it is a major ingredient in many different rocks. Feldspar crystals are often kind of blocky and square.

☐ **Mica** *(say it "my-ka")*
Hardness: 2.5–3

Mica usually forms as very thin, flaky crystals that can be layered together like the pages of a book. Sometimes they are very shiny. Mica is a "rock builder" mineral because it is a very important ingredient in many kinds of rocks.

☐ **Pyroxene** *(say it "pie-rock-seen")*
Hardness: 5–6

Pyroxene is usually black and glassy. It is a "rock builder" mineral because it is a very important ingredient in many kinds of rocks. It can sometimes be seen as little black blocks inside dark rocks.

☐ **Amphibole** *(say it "am-feh-bowl")*
Hardness: 5–6

Amphibole is often black or greenish and can be glassy but also fibrous (like threads). It is another important "rock builder" mineral that is found inside many kinds of rocks. You may find it as little dark, long rectangles inside rocks.

Calcite (say it "kal-site")
Hardness: 3

Calcite is a very common, soft, glassy mineral. It can form in hundreds of different shapes! Many crystals are pointy, but others are blocky and square. It is usually white, but it can also be yellow or brown.

Dolomite (say it "doh-luh-mite")
Hardness: 3.5–4

Dolomite is a common and soft mineral. It looks a lot like calcite but can sometimes be darker colored. Its crystals often look like little blocks, but sometimes they are slightly curved.

Garnet (say it "garr-net")
Hardness: 6.5–7.5

Garnet is a hard mineral that forms in little ball-shaped crystals. They are glassy and can be brown to red in color. Very rare garnets are green. They can sometimes be found in sand, but they will be very small.

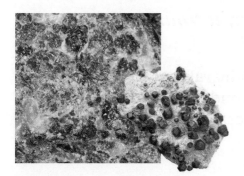

Olivine (say it "olive-een")
Hardness: 6.5–7

Olivine is a common mineral, but it is often so small that you may not notice it! It forms as little glassy green grains inside rocks. Sometimes it can be found in sand if you look very closely.

Common Minerals

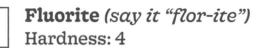

□ **Fluorite** *(say it "flor-ite")*
Hardness: 4

Fluorite is a glassy mineral that can come in many different colors. Its crystals are often blocky with sharp corners, and some are perfect cubes. Most fluorite is translucent, which means that light can shine through it.

□ **Epidote** *(say it "eh-puh-doht")*
Hardness: 6–7

Epidote is almost always dark yellowish green. It forms long glassy crystals. Sometimes you'll find tiny epidote crystals inside the holes in dark-colored rocks.

□ **Tourmaline** *(say it "tour-muh-leen")*
Hardness: 7–7.5

Tourmaline is a glassy mineral that forms long crystals. It can have all kinds of colors, from black to green or pink. It is pretty hard and is often used as a gemstone.

□ **Malachite** *(say it "mal-ah-kite")*
Hardness: 3.5–4

Malachite is a green mineral that has copper in it. It is fairly soft and is usually found as lumpy masses. When a mass of malachite is broken or cut, it may show beautiful layering inside.

Chalcopyrite *(say it "kal-co-pie-rite")*
Hardness: 3.5–4

Chalcopyrite is a shiny metallic mineral that is usually yellow or orange in color. It can form as sharp triangle- or pyramid-shaped crystals. It might look a lot like pyrite, but it is softer and easier to scratch.

Galena *(say it "gah-leen-ah")*
Hardness: 2.5

Galena is a very heavy metallic mineral. It has a gray metal color, but sometimes it can have a tan coating. Its crystals are often shaped like perfect cubes, sometimes clustered together. Galena contains lead, which is bad for you, so avoid handling it.

Talc
Hardness: 1

Talc is the softest mineral, and you can easily scratch it with your fingernails. It is so soft that it almost feels slippery when you hold it, like soap. It is often green and a little shiny.

Serpentine *(say it "ser-pen-teen")*
Hardness: 2.5–4

Serpentine is a soft mineral that is usually green or yellow. It has a greasy luster, so it looks a little bit like it's wet. It is not very common in most places.

Gemstones

Certain minerals are considered special because they are rare and beautiful. These are called **gemstones,** and they are often the most valuable minerals. Most gemstones are translucent, which means that light can shine through them. Gemstones are usually cut and polished so that they can be worn in jewelry.

There are two main groups of gemstones: precious gemstones and semiprecious gemstones. These are not scientific terms, which means that scientists don't really use them. But collectors and jewelers often use these terms, so it's good to know what they mean.

1. Precious gemstones are minerals that are rare, very lustrous (shiny), and very hard. *Precious gemstones are usually between 8 and 10 on the hardness scale.* This makes them tough and good for use in jewelry. They are usually cut to show **facets,** which are little flat areas made at certain angles. Facets make a gemstone look shinier and flashy. There are only a few minerals considered to be precious gems. They are: diamond, ruby, sapphire *(say it "saff-fire"),* emerald, and topaz.

2. Semiprecious gemstones are minerals that are not so rare but can still be very beautiful. Semiprecious gemstones are not worth as much as precious ones, but they are still often used in jewelry. *Semiprecious gemstones are usually between 4 and 7.5 on the hardness scale,* because anything softer is too soft to wear as jewelry. Some are translucent, but others may not be.

Cut diamond gem

Cut sapphire gem

Natural ruby crystals like this are carefully cut to make gems (below) for jewelry.

Cut ruby gem that show its shiny facets that shows its shiny facets

3. Nonprecious stones are minerals that are very common or are too soft to wear as jewelry. They are not considered precious at all. They are often **opaque** (light can't shine through them) or not pretty enough to be used in jewelry. Many metallic minerals are considered to be nonprecious. *Any mineral below a hardness of 4 is too soft to be used in jewelry and is usually not precious.*

Matching: Gemstone Sorting

Using what you've learned about which minerals are used as gemstones, sort these natural and uncut minerals into these categories: precious, semiprecious, or nonprecious.

Many semiprecious gemstones are not cut to have facets, but instead they are cut into cabochons. A **cabochon** is a circle or oval shape that has a rounded top and a flat back. This is an agate cabochon.

1. Garnet
Hardness: 6.5–7.5

2. Diamond
Hardness: 10

3. Emerald
Hardness: 7.5–8

4. Gypsum
Hardness: 2

5. Lapis Lazuli
Hardness: 5–5.5

6. Hematite
Hardness: 5–6

7. Topaz
Hardness: 8

8. Agate
Hardness: 7

Precious	Semiprecious	Nonprecious

Answers on page 119! ☞

Where to Find Minerals

Now that you know all about minerals, you might be wondering where you can find some. Luckily for you, they're everywhere. Minerals form inside rocks, and since rocks are everywhere beneath your feet, you'll have many chances to look for cool crystals.

When you want to find minerals, look in places where there are lots of exposed (uncovered) rocks. That means places like beaches, riverbanks, and even gravel roads where there are lots of rocks to pick up and look at. You won't have as good of luck looking in places like forests where plants and trees cover up most of the rocks.

Sometimes minerals will be found loose on the ground where the weather freed them from the rock they formed in. This happens a lot on beaches. But other times you'll find them still inside the rock. Look for rocks with lots of holes or cracks in them, then carefully look inside.

Just remember to never go out looking for minerals by yourself. Always bring an adult and proper safety supplies, and always watch your step!

If you find soft, light-colored rocks full of holes like this, take a close look inside the holes to see if there are little crystals inside.

This hard dark rock has lots of pockets filled with crystals! They will be very difficult to collect from such hard rock, but you can always take a photo!

On beaches, you may find minerals that have been weathered free of the rock they formed in. This is a pebble of quartz found on a beach. See how the waves made it smooth?

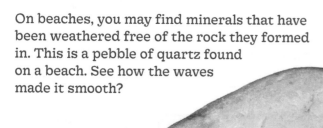

These little topaz crystals are still inside a hole in the rock they formed in.

Rocky beaches are ideal places to look for minerals. Just be careful around the water and waves.

Riverbanks are good places to look because the water pushes lots of rocks around. But be very careful around the moving water.

Exposed rocky areas are great places to look for crystals in the cracks and holes in the rock. Just be very careful because rocks could fall on you.

If you live near a **desert**, it's a great place to look because there aren't a lot of plants to hide the rocks. But never go alone, and always bring drinking water.

Mountainsides are beautiful places to hunt for minerals, but they can be dangerous. Only look for minerals in these areas with an adult's help.

You might see a **cliff** like this and think it's a good spot to look. There may be minerals to find here, but the dirt is too loose and dangerous to risk it.

Rocks

Rocks make up the Earth's surface, and we walk on top of them every day. There are many different kinds of rocks in the world, but they all share one thing in common: all rocks are made of a mixture of minerals, and each kind of rock has a different mixture of minerals in it.

You'll see lots of different kinds of rocks when you're out looking for them. Some have colored speckles, some have thin layers, and some are so soft that they crumble in your hands. But all rocks fall into just three main categories: igneous rocks, sedimentary rocks, and metamorphic rocks.

1. Igneous *(say it "ig-nee-us")* rocks form when the hot magma (melted rock) from inside the Earth cools off and hardens.

2. Sedimentary *(say it "sed-i-ment-air-ee")* rocks form when little pieces of worn-down rocks (like sand) and other materials harden together.

3. Metamorphic *(say it "meh-tuh-mor-fik")* rocks form when igneous or sedimentary rocks are buried deep in the Earth where lots of weight presses on them and the heat inside the Earth softens them, changing them into new rocks.

Basalt *(say it "buh-salt")* is a dark, hard igneous rock formed when melted rock cooled and hardened.

Gneiss *(say it "nice")* is a metamorphic rock that formed when another type of rock, such as granite, was squashed and heated deep in the Earth. This process changed it and gave it speckly layers.

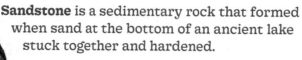

Sandstone is a sedimentary rock that formed when sand at the bottom of an ancient lake stuck together and hardened.

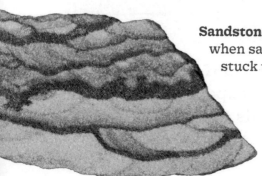

Igneous Rocks

Igneous rocks are formed when hot, melted rocks cool down and harden. This can happen deep inside the Earth's crust as well as on the Earth's surface, such as at a volcano.

Remember that it is very hot deep inside the Earth—so hot that it can melt rocks! The melted rock inside the Earth is called **magma**, and it moves and flows very slowly beneath the Earth's crust. When it gets pushed up into the crust, it can begin to cool down and harden. But it usually cools very slowly, sometimes taking thousands of years to become a hard rock.

Sometimes magma can be pushed up into the crust so far that it breaks the surface. This is called a vent, or a **volcano**. When magma is pushed out of the Earth and spills out over the ground, then we call it **lava**. Lava is red-hot, but it can cool off and harden very quickly when it hits the cold air. Once hardened, it is a rock.

When lava comes out of a volcano, lots of gas and ash (a combination of crushed rock, glass, and minerals) come out with it. This is called an **eruption**. Igneous rocks that form deep in the Earth when magma cooled slowly are very different from igneous rocks that formed on the Earth's surface and cooled quickly after an eruption.

Andesite *(say it "an-dih-zite")* is a type of igneous rock that formed when lava cooled very quickly during an eruption.

Pegmatite *(say it "peg-muh-tite")* is a kind of rock that formed very deep inside the Earth when magma cooled extremely slowly.

Igneous Rock Formation

Igneous rocks can form when melted rock cools off either inside the Earth or on the Earth's surface, after an eruption. But the depth at which magma or lava cools can make a big difference for what kind of rock will be formed.

You can think of magma as being like a "soup" of minerals, all blended together. But the same magma can make different kinds of rocks depending on where it cools. When magma cools very deep in the Earth, it takes a very long time, and the minerals inside the magma have a long time to turn into crystals. This creates rocks that have large mineral grains in them, and they look speckly or spotted. Granite is a good example. But rocks that formed when lava cooled very quickly on the Earth's surface had very little time for their minerals to form, so the mineral grains are very small. Usually, you won't see many speckled colors on igneous rocks that cooled very quickly. This is called **grain size**, and it's important for identifying rocks.

The rocks on the right all formed from magma or lava that had the same mixture of minerals in it. The only difference is how deep in the Earth they cooled!

A. Gabbro

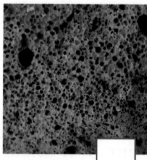
B. Scoria

C. Basalt

Ordering: Grain Size

These four rocks on the right all contain the same basic mixture of minerals. The only difference is how fast they cooled. But they are out of order! First, study the pictures and descriptions on the next page. Then, using what you've learned about the grain size of igneous rocks, number these rocks in the correct order from 1 to 4, with 1 being the rock that cooled the slowest and 4 being the rock that cooled the fastest.

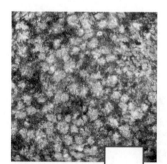
D. Diabase

Answers on page 119! ☞

Pumice: Lava has lots of gases in it that rise to the top. Pumice formed when lava at the very top of an eruption cooled very quickly. It has lots of gas bubbles in it. It's a lot like the bubbles at the top of a glass of fizzy soda!

Rhyolite: Rhyolite formed when lava cooled on or very near the Earth's surface. This means it cooled quickly and the minerals in it didn't have a lot of time to grow into large crystals. It usually has very small grains that you can just barely see.

Granite: Granite formed when magma down in the Earth cooled slowly. The minerals in it had lots of time to grow and turn into crystals. Granite is usually speckly with different colors, because each color is a different mineral that grew big enough to see!

Pegmatite: Very deep in the Earth, magma can take thousands of years to cool. This can make the crystals in the magma grow to very large sizes. Pegmatite is a type of rock made of very large crystals that grew together very slowly.

Sedimentary Rocks

Sedimentary rocks form when **particles** (tiny pieces) called sediments stick together and harden. **Sediments** are tiny pieces of sand, silt, clay, mud, and even plant and animal remains, such as coral. Sedimentary rocks form entirely on the Earth's surface (or underwater), while the other kinds of rocks form as a result of the magma, heat, and pressure from inside the Earth.

Sedimentary rocks can have many layers. Each layer formed from year after year of sediments sinking to the bottom of a sea.

When rocks are exposed to water and wind for too long, they start to crumble and wear away. This is called weathering, and it can break lots of tiny pieces off the rock to become sediments like sand. With enough time, even whole mountains can be worn down to sand. Sand and other sediments are very lightweight, so water can move them around easily. Rivers can wash sediments into lakes and oceans, where they sink and settle to the bottom. After a long time, thick layers of sediments can begin to harden together and become a rock.

Sedimentary rocks are not usually as hard as igneous rocks or metamorphic rocks. Some sedimentary rocks are even so soft that you can break them with your bare hands. Many have lots of little layers that will easily split apart, and many will feel kind of gritty or chalky in your hands.

Limestone: Ancient coral reefs often became limestone. Limestone is soft and chalky, and it can contain fossils of sea life in it.

Sandstone: Sand at the bottom of ancient lakes and seas hardened to become sandstone. Sandstone is usually rough and grainy, and you can often pick little sand grains right off the rock.

Shale: Mud at the bottom of calm ancient seas became shale. Shale is soft and forms in flaky layers that can be separated, almost like big sheets of paper.

Sedimentary Rock Formation

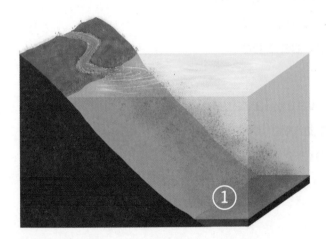

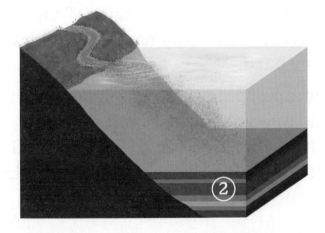

1. Sediments, like sand and silt, wash into lakes and seas and begin to sink and settle on the bottom in a big layer called a bed.

2. After a long time, many different layers of different kinds of sediments can build up. The deepest ones can start to harden together to become a sedimentary rock.

Metamorphic Rocks

Metamorphic rocks form when old rocks are turned into new kinds of rocks through a process called metamorphism. **Metamorphism** happens when rocks are heated up, squashed by lots of weight, or both.

When rocks become deeply buried down where the Earth is hot, they can be heated up and partially melted. This softens the rock, and many changes can happen to the rock's minerals when that happens. When the rock cools off again, it won't be the same kind of rock because the heat changed it too much. Then we call it a metamorphic rock.

Similarly, when a rock is buried deep in the ground, all the weight of the rocks and dirt above it press down on it very hard. This can squash the rock so much that it changes. Lots of metamorphic rocks that form this way have tiny layers that can be very hard.

Metamorphic rocks can have colorful wavy layers and speckled colors, and they can also have lots of glittery minerals in them. Many valuable gemstones also form inside metamorphic rocks.

Metamorphic rocks can have lots of tight, wavy layers from being squeezed by tons of weight.

Marble: When limestone is heated and pressed by lots of weight, it turns into marble. Marble can be very white and has little shiny crystals all over in it.

Answers on page 119! ☞

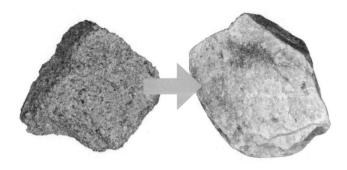

Quartzite: When sandstone is heated and pressed by lots of weight, it can become quartzite. Quartzite is much harder than sandstone, and you can't separate the grains of sand anymore.

Slate: When shale has been pressed by lots of weight for a long time, it forms a tightly layered, hard rock called slate.

Metamorphic Rock Formation

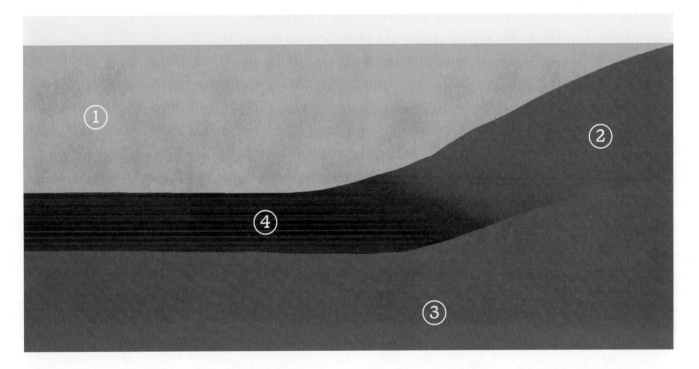

1. Rock layers that are higher up in the Earth press down on the rocks deeper below.

2. As this layer of rock gets buried deeper, the weight above it and heat below it will change it more and more.

3. Heat from deep in the Earth can soften the rocks above it.

4. This rock layer is being pressed from above and heated from below. It is changing into metamorphic rock.

Sediments

When rocks and minerals weather and break down, they become little pieces called sediments. And the more they wear down, the smaller the sediments get. Sediments can be carried by flowing water, like a river, and end up in lakes and seas where they eventually sink. Some large sediments sink very quickly, settling to the bottom in a short amount of time, but some tiny sediments sink very slowly and can take a long time to finally settle. When sediments build up at the bottom of a lake or sea, we call it a bed. And when the bed becomes thick enough, it can begin to harden and turn into a sedimentary rock.

Not all sediments came from rocks and minerals, though. Some are made by plants and animals! Coral reefs, like the ones alive in the oceans today, can become so big and thick that the coral (and other shells) at the bottom can start to turn into rock. Limestone often forms in this way and is very common around the world.

Ancient **coral reefs**, made by living coral and other sea life, became a special kind of sediment that turned into limestone.

Gravel is one of the largest kinds of sediments. Each grain in gravel is a small pebble that you can easily pick up individually. Gravel sinks very quickly and settles first.

Sand is a kind of sediment with grains smaller than gravel. Sand is the kind of sediment you usually find on a beach. Sand grains are pretty small, but you can still pick up individual grains. Sand sinks and settles pretty fast.

Silt is a sediment with tiny grains. The grains are so small you can barely see them individually, and you couldn't pick up just one grain. Silt often looks like smooth, soft mud. It can take a while for silt to sink and settle.

Clay is the tiniest sediment. The grains are so small that they are microscopic! Each grain is even smaller than the period at the end of this sentence. Clay can hold lots of water and be sticky when wet. Clay can take days to sink and settle.

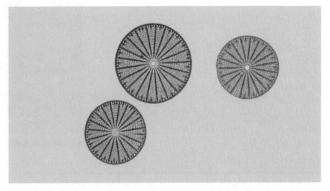

Diatoms are a form of tiny ocean life that grow tiny skeletons made of a material like quartz. These ones are shown under a microscope. When lots and lots of diatoms die, they sink to the bottom and can later form the rock called chert.

Activity: Sediment Settling

You can see for yourself how different-sized sediments settle at different speeds.

What you'll need:

- A large jar with a tight-fitting lid
- Water
- Dirt or soil from outside

1. Fill a large jar about ⅔ full with water.

2. Put a few handfuls of dirt into the jar—be careful not the make the jar overflow.

3. Put the lid on tightly and shake the jar to mix up the dirt.

4. Set the jar down and don't move it any more. Now watch what happens.

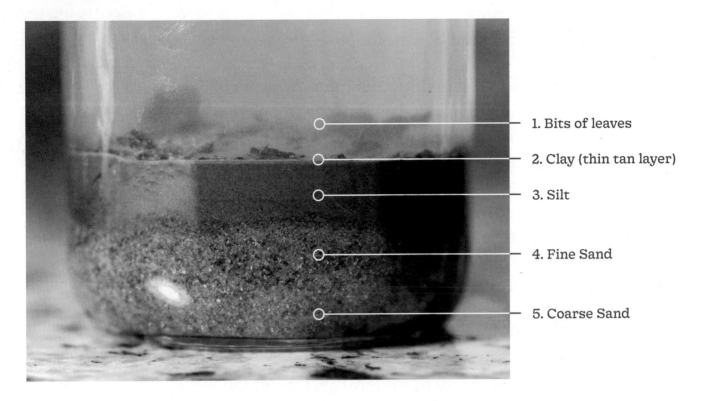

1. Bits of leaves
2. Clay (thin tan layer)
3. Silt
4. Fine Sand
5. Coarse Sand

You'll see the heavy sand sink to the bottom very quickly, in just a few seconds.

Above the heavy, coarse sand at the bottom, you'll then see another layer of finer sand start to settle in the next 30 seconds or so.

After an hour, you'll see that some really fine-grained sediments have settled. That's silt, and it takes longer to settle than the sand because it's smaller and lighter.

After a full day, you'll see that the water will have gotten clearer, and another layer will have settled. The last layer is clay, and it is made of sediment so tiny that it takes a long time to sink and settle.

You may see different kinds of layers when you do this activity. That's because not all dirt has the same mixture of sand, silt, and clay. If you use dirt from a forest or a garden for this experiment, it will most likely be a soil that may take a little longer to settle.

Rock Properties

All three of the categories of rocks have properties that can make them easier to identify. A **property** of a rock is a characteristic or trait, such as how hard it is or if it has colored layers or not. Below are some of the key properties of each category of rock. Not all kinds of rocks that fall within these categories will have all of these properties, but many will, so they are important to know when you're trying to identify rocks.

An example of an igneous rock: basalt

Properties of Igneous Rocks

- Most igneous rocks are hard and tough.
- Igneous rocks are made up of mineral grains, which are sometimes large enough to see and give rocks a speckly, spotted appearance.
- If you look very closely, the mineral grains in igneous rocks are usually jagged and angular.
- Some igneous rocks can show lots of little round gas bubbles trapped in them.
- Many igneous rocks are dark colored, but others may have spots of different colors.
- Many igneous rocks don't show much layering, if at all.

Properties of Sedimentary Rocks

- Many sedimentary rocks are fairly soft and are easily rounded by water and wind.
- Some sedimentary rocks are layered. Some have flaky, soft layers that can be pulled apart.
- Many sedimentary rocks have a gritty or chalky texture and may feel kind of dusty.

An example of a sedimentary rock: limestone

- If you look very closely, you may be able to see that the grains in sedimentary rocks are often rounded.
- Many sedimentary rocks are soft enough that you can pick little pieces off them with just your hands.
- Many sedimentary rocks are light colored, such as gray, white, yellow, or tan.
- Some sedimentary rocks may have fossils inside, which look like pieces of animals and plants, such as curved shells or sharp teeth.

An example of a metamorphic rock: schist

Properties of Metamorphic Rocks

- Most metamorphic rocks are fairly hard.
- Some metamorphic rocks are layered, but the layers are often thin and tightly stuck together.
- Sometimes the layers in metamorphic rocks can be curved or wavy.
- Many metamorphic rocks are speckly colors; even their colored layers may be kind of speckly and multicolored.
- Some metamorphic rocks may have a glittery or sparkly appearance because of flaky mica minerals inside them.
- If you look very closely, you may be able to see that the mineral grains in metamorphic rocks are often flat.
- Metamorphic rocks can be many different colors, sometimes even within the same piece. Many are black, gray, or white, but others can have pink, green, or yellow too.

Quiz Time

1. Of the three kinds of rocks, which ones are usually the softest?

_____

2. What kind of rock can have round bubbles in it?

_____

3. Some metamorphic rocks can look glittery because of which mineral in them?

_____

Answers on page 119! ☞

Matching: Rock Properties

Now that you've learned about the three categories of rocks, use what you know to figure out if these rocks are igneous, sedimentary, or metamorphic. Look carefully at their properties and draw a line to the label that you think best describes these rocks.

1. Limestone

2. Argillite

3 Gneiss

4. Schist

5. Basalt

6. Granodiorite

7. Pegmatite

8. Sandstone

9. Slate

Igneous   **Sedimentary**   **Metamorphic**

Answers on page 119! ☞

The Rock Cycle

Rocks may seem hard and solid, but none of them will last forever. Rocks are always changing. The rain and wind weathers them and breaks them down into sand, heavy layers of rock can make pressure that squashes the lower layers and changes them, and rocks that are buried deep in the Earth can melt and become new kinds of rocks. An igneous rock today may become a metamorphic rock many millions of years from now, and millions of years after that, all may be left of it are sediments, like sand.

The way that rocks can be changed and turned into other kinds of rocks is called the rock cycle. The **rock cycle** is the way rocks change over time, and it never stops! The diagram on the next two pages will help you understand the rock cycle.

The rock cycle shows us how one kind of rock can change into a completely different kind. And a lot of these changes happen because of how hot the Earth is inside—hot enough to melt rocks! The red-hot melted rocks move around slowly, flowing like thick syrup, and change the Earth's crust above them. Volcanoes like this one remind us that even the ground beneath our feet isn't as solid as it seems!

The Rock Cycle

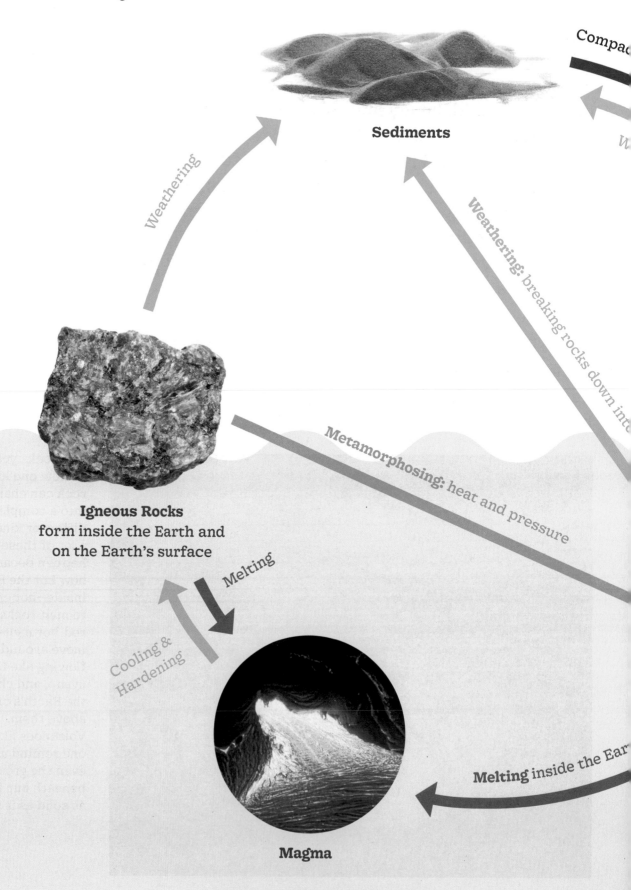

On the Surface

Inside the Earth

Sediments

Compac...

Weathering

Weathering: breaking rocks down into

Metamorphosing: heat and pressure

Igneous Rocks
form inside the Earth and
on the Earth's surface

Melting

Cooling &
Hardening

Melting inside the Eart...

Magma

dening

Sedimentary Rocks
form on or near the
Earth's surface

Metamorphosing

Metamorphic Rocks
form inside the Earth

Quiz Time: Rock Cycle

Using what you've learned
about the rock cycle, answer
these questions:

1. How does a metamorphic
rock eventually turn into an
igneous rock?

_____

_____

2. Would a sedimentary rock
be able to melt deep inside the
Earth, or would it have to change
into another kind of rock first?

_____

_____

3. Which type of rock forms only
when buried inside the Earth?

_____

4. After a rock melts, it can only
harden into one type of rock.
What type is it?

_____

5. What types of rocks
can be weathered down
to form sediments?

_____

Answers on page 119! ☞

Common Rocks

While igneous, sedimentary, and metamorphic rocks are the three major rock types, there are lots of individual kinds of rocks that fit into those categories. Each of these rocks has a different mixture of minerals, a different grain size, different textures and colors, and—most importantly—they formed in completely different ways. You can use this list to learn about the most common kinds of rocks and check them off once you've found them.

Basalt
(say it "buh-salt")

Basalt is an igneous rock that formed when lava cooled quickly on the Earth's surface. It has very small mineral grains and is usually dark colored because it has lots of iron in it. Some basalt can have lots of air bubbles in it.

Gabbro
(say it "gab-bro")

Gabbro is a dark, heavy igneous rock that formed deep in the Earth. It's a lot like basalt, but has large mineral grains and crystals in it. It is usually dark colored, and sometimes greenish.

Granite
(say it "gra-nit")

Granite is a very common igneous rock that formed deep in the ground when magma cooled very slowly. It has big, chunky mineral grains in it that give it a speckled look.

☐ Rhyolite
(say it "rye-uh-lite")

Rhyolite is a lighter-colored igneous rock that formed when lava cooled quickly on the Earth's surface. It's very similar to granite, but it didn't cool inside the Earth. It can have air bubbles trapped in it, just like basalt.

☐ Tuff

Tuff is a different kind of igneous rock because it didn't form from magma or lava. Instead, it formed when ash (rock dust) from volcanic eruptions hardened together to make a rock. It is usually light colored and can contain little bits of natural glass.

☐ Chert

Chert is a very hard sedimentary rock that formed when trillions of tiny skeletons of microscopic sea life settled to the bottom of the ocean and hardened together over time. It's common in rivers and beaches.

☐ Conglomerate
(say it "kuhn-glom-uh-rut")

Conglomerate is a neat kind of sedimentary rock because it contains sediments of different sizes. Big, rounded pebbles from ancient rivers are cemented together by a fine-grained material that locks the pebbles in place.

Common Rocks

☐ Limestone

Limestone is a very common sedimentary rock that often formed when ancient coral reefs turned into rock. That makes limestone like a fossil of the sea floor! Sometimes bigger fossils, like clams or coral, can be found inside of it.

☐ Mudstone

Just like its name sounds, mudstone formed when mud hardened into a sedimentary rock! It has very fine grains of sediment in it that are much smaller than grains of sand.

☐ Sandstone

Sandstone is a sedimentary rock formed when sand stuck together and hardened. It is a gritty, coarse rock, and sometimes you can even get grains of sand to come off of it.

☐ Shale

Shale is a soft sedimentary rock with lots of layers. It is made of mud and clay, just like mudstone, but the main difference is that shale has many layers. Many times, you can split apart the layers in shale—look for fossils in between the layers!

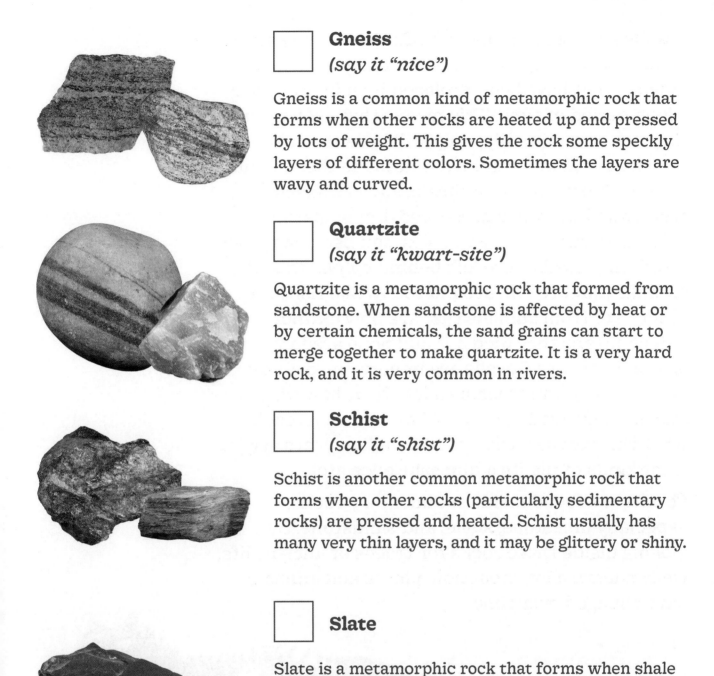

Gneiss
(say it "nice")

Gneiss is a common kind of metamorphic rock that forms when other rocks are heated up and pressed by lots of weight. This gives the rock some speckly layers of different colors. Sometimes the layers are wavy and curved.

Quartzite
(say it "kwart-site")

Quartzite is a metamorphic rock that formed from sandstone. When sandstone is affected by heat or by certain chemicals, the sand grains can start to merge together to make quartzite. It is a very hard rock, and it is very common in rivers.

Schist
(say it "shist")

Schist is another common metamorphic rock that forms when other rocks (particularly sedimentary rocks) are pressed and heated. Schist usually has many very thin layers, and it may be glittery or shiny.

Slate

Slate is a metamorphic rock that forms when shale is compressed and heated up in the Earth. It has hard, thin, brittle layers that may easily break apart. It is usually dark colored.

Fossils

Fossils are traces of ancient life that are preserved inside rocks. They are parts of dead plants and animals that have been replaced by minerals over a long period of time. This means that even though they are now minerals, they still have the shape of the ancient plant or animal that made them. Usually only the hard parts of animals, such as shells, teeth, and bones, are preserved, but sometimes soft materials, like plant leaves, can become fossils too. Some fossils were left behind by plants and animals that are still around today, like fish, but others are from animals that are now **extinct** (which means they died out and none are left), such as the dinosaurs. Fossils are important to study because they can teach us a lot about how plants and animals lived long ago. They can even teach us what the weather was like 100 million years ago, or what kinds of plants a dinosaur once ate!

Fossils are found inside sedimentary rocks, especially limestone, shale, and sandstone. By looking inside these rocks for traces of ancient life, we can learn a lot about how plants and animals have changed over time.

Tyrannosaurs rex fossil

Fossil Dig: The dinosaur bones in this photo show how they look when scientists find them. They're often mixed up and flattened. Sometimes parts of a dinosaur skeleton are missing, too, especially the head or tail. Bones like this must be very carefully chiseled out of the rock.

Trilobite *(say it "try-luh-bite")*: This strange fossil is a trilobite. It may look like a bug, but trilobites were ancient animals that lived in the oceans. They were around for over 200 million years, but they are extinct now.

Seashells: Dinosaur fossils are very rare, but other fossils are quite common! Fossils of sea life, especially ones with shells, like snails and clams, are abundant and can be easy to find (if you're in the right place)!

Plants: Plant fossils can be found in certain kinds of rocks too. Lots of plants were too soft to turn into a fossil, but in the right conditions, some were preserved in shale.

How Do Fossils Form?

But how did the remains of plants and animals turn into minerals trapped inside rocks? One of the main ways it happened went like this: Long ago, when an animal died, it was buried in sediment where it could not **decay**, or rot away, like it usually would. As the sediments started to harden and turn into a rock, minerals in the groundwater soaked into the animal's bones and started to grow tiny crystals. This replaced the bones with minerals little by little. Eventually, when the sediments had hardened and become a rock, the bones inside had also hardened into minerals and become part of the rock. This is called **fossilization**.

Sometimes an ancient plant or animal was too fragile to be fossilized this way. But if we're lucky, we can still find fossils of them. When they were buried in sediment, their soft bodies pressed into the mud or silt, leaving an **impression** behind. An impression is a hole left in the rock in the shape of an ancient plant or animal. Impressions can still show us what ancient life looked like even though the plant or animal isn't there anymore!

Fossil **fish** are pretty common around the world. This one was so well preserved in the rock that you can see not only its bones, but even its scales!

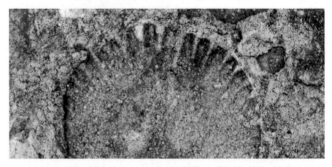

It may look like there's a seashell in this rock, but actually it's only an **impression** of one! That means the shell isn't there anymore, but its shape was pressed into the rock.

Fossil Formation

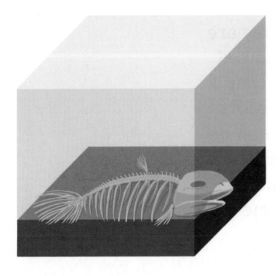

1. After this fish died, it sank to the bottom of the lake.

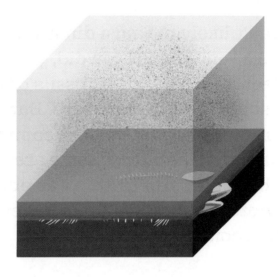

2. Over time, it was buried by sediment. Often this happened quickly in a landslide.

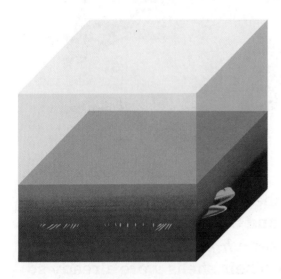

3. After it was completely buried, the weight of the mud began to press on the bones. Minerals in the water started to soak into the bones and begin fossilizing it.

4. A long time later, when the lake dried up, all the sediments turned into rock, and the fossil bones were trapped inside the sedimentary rock layers.

Common Fossils

You aren't likely to find a dinosaur fossil—they are very rare—and even if you did, you aren't allowed to collect it. In fact, most fossils of animals that have backbones are quite rare. But there are lots of fossils that are much more common and can be found all over the world. Some are recognizable, like snail shells. But others aren't as obvious, and you might not know they're a fossil! Here are some of the most common fossils that you could find.

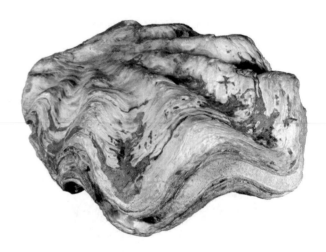

Snails are small, soft animals that don't fossilize, but their hard shells do! Their shells are common in limestone and chert and you could even find one; look for their little spiral shapes.

Hard-shelled sea creatures like **clams and brachiopods** (*say it "bray-kee-uh-pod"*) are also common fossils. Their shells were already so hard when they were alive that they easily turned into fossils.

Trilobites were ancient sea creatures that crawled along the seafloor. They had hard, segmented bodies with lots of little joints. They are all extinct today.

Ammonite shells may look like snail shells, but they're not! Ammonites were an animal like a squid, but they had a hard, spiral shell.

Triceratops fossil

Quiz Time

1. What is the process of a bone turning into a fossil called?

_____

2. Fossils are almost always found in only one of the three categories of rocks—which one?

_____

3. Fossil bones in a rock aren't made of bone anymore. Instead, they've been replaced by:

_____

Answers on page 119! ☞

Common Fossils

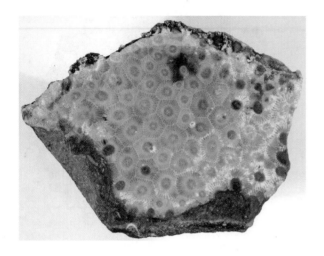

Coral fossils are very common, and you may find them on beaches or along rivers. They look like honeycomb or fabric-like shapes in rocks.

Fossilized trees and wood are called **petrified wood**. It is very common and can often be found on beaches. It can look just like wood, and even have tree bark, but it's all rock now!

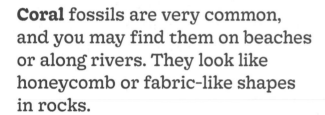

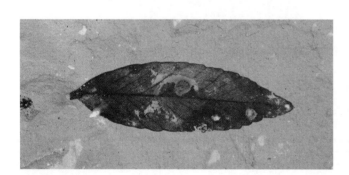

In general, **leaves** are too soft to fossilize. But in the right places, we can find them, especially in between the layers in shale.

Ferns were once a lot more common than they are today, so there are lots of fossils of them. Some fern fossils can even be found in coal.

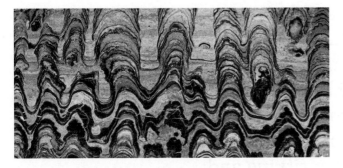

Stromatolites were one of the first living things on Earth, and they're still around today! They are a type of bacteria that grow in lumpy, wavy stacks that were easily preserved in rock. They are found all over the world.

You might find limestone with lots of little circle or tube shapes in it. Those are **crinoid** stems! Crinoids are a sea creature that has a long stem that anchors it to rocks. When they died, their stems fell apart and were fossilized.

Quiz Time

1. Fossils can teach us about ancient animals that aren't around anymore, like dinosaurs. What happened to them?

_____

2. Dinosaur fossils are very rare, but fish, snails, clams, and trilobite fossils are common. What do those types of animals have in common?

_____

Answers on page 119! ☞

Identifying Fossils

When scientists find a fossil, they have to figure out what plant or animal made it. They can do this by comparing it to plants and animals that are still alive today. Lots of creatures that were alive millions of years ago are still alive today, so their fossils don't look very different from the living thing. This can be very helpful for identifying and studying ancient life. Here are some comparisons of plants and animals that still look a lot like they did millions of years ago:

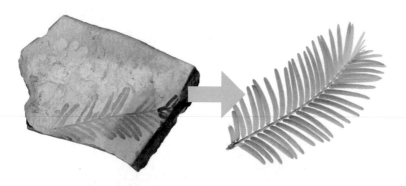

Sequoia: The leaves of this ancient fossil *Sequoia* tree look a lot like a leaf from a *Sequoia* living today.

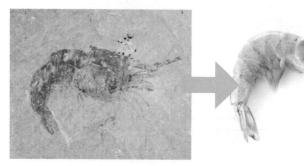

Shrimp: Shrimp are ancient sea creatures, and their fossils can look just like living shrimp.

Starfish: See how little starfish have changed over millions of years? Fossil starfish look just like living ones.

Matching: Modern to Ancient Life

These four photos show plants and animals that are alive today. But they have relatives that lived millions of years ago, which we can find as fossils. Try to match the living thing (top) to the fossil that best matches it (bottom). What is different between the ancient and living plants and animals? What is the same?

Modern: Living

 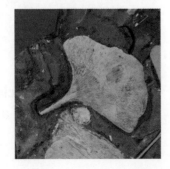  

1. *Ginkgo* Tree Leaf (plant)

2. Crinoid (animal)

3. Frog (animal)

4. Bluegill Fish (animal)

Ancient: Fossils

A.

B.

C.

D.

  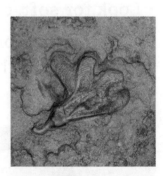 

E.

F.

G.

H.

Answers on page 119! ☞

Where to Find Fossils

If you want to find fossils of your own, you need to look in the right kinds of places. They can also take a lot of work and patience to find.

Much like when you're looking for minerals, you'll have better luck finding fossils in places where there are lots of exposed (uncovered) rocks. This makes cliffs, beaches, and even gravel roads good places to look. But remember that fossils are pretty much only found in sedimentary rocks, primarily shale, limestone, and sandstone, so it would be a good idea to learn how to identify those kinds of rocks.

Here are some things to watch out for when looking for rocks with fossils:

- Check light-colored, soft rocks; lots of sedimentary rocks are gray or tan.

- Look for rocks with lots of flaky layers.

- Look for soft, chalky rocks with lots of little holes.

- Check rocks for odd stripes, circles, patterns, or little curves—they may be parts of fossils.

Layered Rocks: When you see lots of flat rock layers like this, you've probably found a sedimentary rock formation! Look carefully between the layers in the rock for fossils.

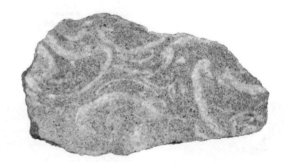

Sandstone: The little curving shapes in this sandstone are actually the edges of fossil shells.

Beaches: Some beaches may have lots of fossils hidden in the sand and pebbles. Look carefully in the rocks for patterns that look like they could be shells or coral.

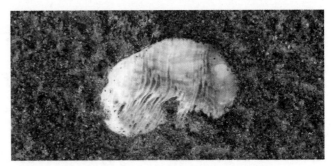

Petrified Wood: Sometimes you can find hard pieces of petrified wood on beaches. This piece is still in the sand and has been rounded by the waves.

Shale: These flaky shale cliffs are perfect places to hunt for fossils. Just be careful of falling rock! Shale is one of the best rocks to look in for fossils.

Its flaky layers are often so soft that you can easily split them apart, almost like sheets of paper. You can look between the layers for fossils, like these fish.

Limestone: Limestone is one of the most common rocks to find fossils in. But sometimes they may not look like a fossil right away. Pay attention to the shapes you see in limestone, and any that look like spirals, stripes, or circles

may actually be fossils! If you need help figuring it out, find a guidebook that will show you the fossils in your area. This white limestone shows a few different fossils. *Can you see part of a snail shell?*

Mountains, Valleys, and Plateaus

Some of the most impressive landforms that you'll see throughout the world are mountains, valleys, and plateaus. From the high peaks of mountains to the low rivers in valleys, let's look at how tectonic plates and weathering make these landforms.

Mountains are rocks that rise high above the rest of the land. Most mountains form when two tectonic plates crash into each other, pushing one up over the other. Younger mountains are higher and pointier, while old mountains are lower and rounded.

A **valley** is a low area between two mountains. They often form when water flows down the mountains and collects between them in a river. After a long time, the river washes away the rock and widens the gap between the mountains.

Plateaus *(say it "plah-tohs")* are large flat areas that are higher than the surrounding land. They usually have steep cliffs on some of their sides. They can form when tectonic plates push rock upward, or when water washes away nearby rocks.

A **butte** *(say it "byoot")* is kind of like a plateau, because it has a flat top and high, steep sides, but is much smaller than a plateau. They are usually made of sedimentary rocks and formed when weathering wore away the surrounding rock.

Activity: Make Your Own Rivers and Lakes

With just some sand and water, you can see how moving water, like a river, can make all sorts of landforms.

What you'll need:

- Sand
- Water
- A pan or other flat container, such as aluminum foil bent into a pan shape

1. Put some sand in a pan or other flat container and tilt it slightly to form a "hill."

Note: This is a great activity to try at the beach! Try making little hills of sand, then slowly pour water down the sides and see how it moves the sand around to make little rivers, valleys, and canyons.

2. Slowly trickle some water onto the top of the "hill" and let it run down toward the bottom. Keep doing this until a little river starts to form. Watch how the water easily moves the sand grains.

Experiment with differently shaped hills, or hills that are more or less steep. Try putting some hard rocks in the sand too. Watch how all of these things can change how the water flows and create different landforms.

Caves and Sinkholes

Caves and sinkholes are both landforms that are made when water dissolves soft rocks, which causes them to collapse, forming a hole in the ground.

Here's how it happens.

Caves can form in a few different ways, but most caves are formed in limestone. Limestone is easily dissolved by acids. When groundwater containing acid soaks into limestone, it begins to dissolve it. After a long time, so much limestone can dissolve and wash away that a big opening will be left behind. This is called a cave, or cavern. They are dark places that oftentimes still have lots of water in them.

In a limestone cave, you may see lots of icicle-shaped rocks hanging down from the ceiling. These are called **stalactites**, and they form when water that has minerals in it drips from the ceiling. As the water drips in, the minerals stick to the ceiling and slowly form a stalactite, drip by drip. Sometimes below a stalactite is another kind of mineral structure that goes upward. This is called a **stalagmite**, and it forms when water from a stalactite drips in the same spot for a long time. Eventually, they can touch and connect!

Sinkholes also form when groundwater dissolves limestone. Sometimes a cave can have a thin, weak roof that collapses and falls, leaving a deep hole in the ground. This is called a sinkhole, and they can be small or big. Some are so big that they can make whole buildings fall into the ground!

Some special sinkholes have pools of groundwater at the bottom. These are called **cenotes** *(say it "sih-noh-tee")*, and they can be very beautiful because they are often found in tropical areas. Sometimes the water at the bottom is very deep and can connect to other underwater caves.

Cave and Sinkhole Formation

1. This big cave may eventually turn into a sinkhole if the roof becomes too weak.

2. This small cave formed when water dissolved the limestone.

3. This is a cenote. It is a big, deep sinkhole with water at the bottom.

Activity: Make Your Own Cave

To see how water can dissolve rocks underground to make a cave, try this activity!

What you'll need:

- Non-drying modeling clay
- Sugar cubes
- A clear glass jar big enough to fit your hand in
- Water
- A straw, small funnel, or an eyedropper

---

1. Make a stack of sugar cubes inside a jar, up against the side of the glass.

---

2. Push clay against the back of the sugar cubes. You can put as much clay around the cubes as you like, but leave a small hole at the top.

3. Use the straw or eyedropper to slowly drip water into the hole in the clay. Watch what happens to the sugar cubes!

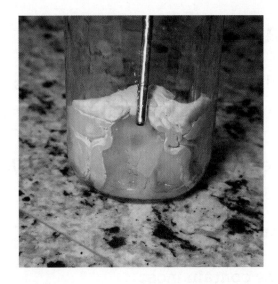

4. After a while, the sugar cubes will start to dissolve and leave behind a cave! This is a lot like how limestone caves form in nature.

The sugar cubes represent limestone, which can be dissolved. The clay represents other rocks that aren't easily dissolved.

Oceans, Lakes, and Rivers

Bodies of water, like oceans, lakes, and rivers, are amazing natural places, but they all formed in different ways.

From the wide oceans to small lakes, let's look at how all that water got to where it is.

Oceans are huge, salty bodies of water that separate the continents of Earth. The oceans contain most of the water on Earth and a huge amount of all life. Oceans form when tectonic plates spread apart from each other. This can make a gap between them, and magma rises up to fill the space with new rock. And since the continents sit on top of the tectonic plates, when the plates spread apart, the continents do, too. Eventually, the space between the continents will start to collect water. And when it gets really big and has collected lots of water, it becomes an ocean.

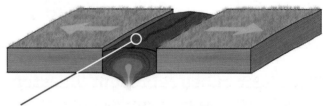

Eventually, an ocean can form between two plates that are spreading apart.

Lakes are smaller bodies of water that form in low spots on the Earth. Since water flows downhill and collects in lower areas, lakes can form wherever there is a low spot and enough water to fill it. In North America, many lakes are found in mountains and in northern regions, and there are fewer lakes in hot, dry regions. The water in nearly all lakes is fresh, not salt like in the oceans, but there are exceptions, such as the Great Salt Lake in Utah.

Many lakes around the world were made by glaciers. Glaciers are huge sheets of ice that move very slowly. When glaciers begin to melt, they can break up, leaving huge blocks of ice behind. The blocks are so big that they can take years to melt, and they collect dirt and gravel (sediments) around them as they do. Eventually, this can leave a hole in the ground where a lake can form. This is called a **kettle lake** and is one of the most common kinds of lakes.

A glacier is a huge, thick sheet of ice that slowly moves across the land.

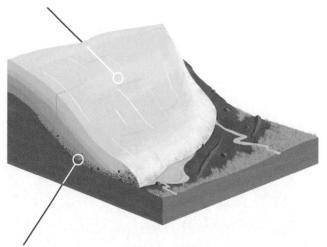

Lots of sediment is picked up by the glacier and trapped in the ice until it melts.

Oceans, Lakes, and Rivers

A **river** is a path that water takes as it flows downhill. Rivers follow channels, or grooves, that are carved deeper by the water. Rivers can form in a low spot between landforms, like in a valley between mountains, but they can also form in wide-open areas. Where a river is found also affects the speed of the river. Steep areas, like in hills or mountains, make for fast rivers that are straighter. Flat areas, like plains, make for very slow rivers that are more winding and curvy.

Quiz Time

1. When a cave has a weak roof, it can collapse and fall in. What's this called?

_____

2. Name two kinds of landforms that have high, flat tops.

_____

3. What can be found in groundwater that will slowly dissolve rocks?

_____

Answers on page 119! ☞

Activity: Make Your Own Kettle Lake

To see how a kettle lake is made by a giant piece of a melting glacier, you can make one at home!

What you'll need:
- Sand
- Water
- An ice cube

---

1. Start by filling a small dish or pan with sand, then carefully pour some water into the sand to make it wet. Don't pour in too much water—you just want the sand to be damp to the touch. *This represents the damp sediments left behind by the glacier.*

---

2. Push an ice cube into the sand and bury it more than halfway. *This represents a huge block of ice that has broken off a melting glacier and become trapped in the sediments.*

---

3. Wait patiently for the ice cube to melt. Then look at what's left behind. Do you see a bowl-shaped indentation in the sand? *This represents a kettle lake.*

Volcanoes

When magma deep inside the Earth is pushed upward, it can sometimes break the surface of the Earth's crust and spill out. The place where it comes through the surface is a vent called a volcano. When magma comes out of a volcano, we call it an eruption. And after the magma flows out onto the Earth's surface, we then call the red-hot molten rock lava. Along with lava, lots of gas and crushed rock called ash also comes out of a volcano during an eruption. As soon as lava comes out of a volcano, it begins to cool and harden to form igneous rocks.

Some volcanoes are big cone-shaped mountains, which form when lots of eruptions build up rocks around the vent. But other volcanoes are just cracks or holes in the ground where lava oozes out slowly. In all volcanoes, the molten rock rises up because pressure deep inside the Earth pushes it. It's like squeezing a bottle of water, then suddenly taking off the cap—the water will shoot out because of the pressure of your squeezing hands!

Some eruptions are very explosive! This cone-shaped volcano is spewing lava and gas into the air.

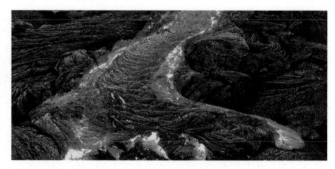

Other eruptions are slow and can just ooze lava over the land.

Inside a Volcano

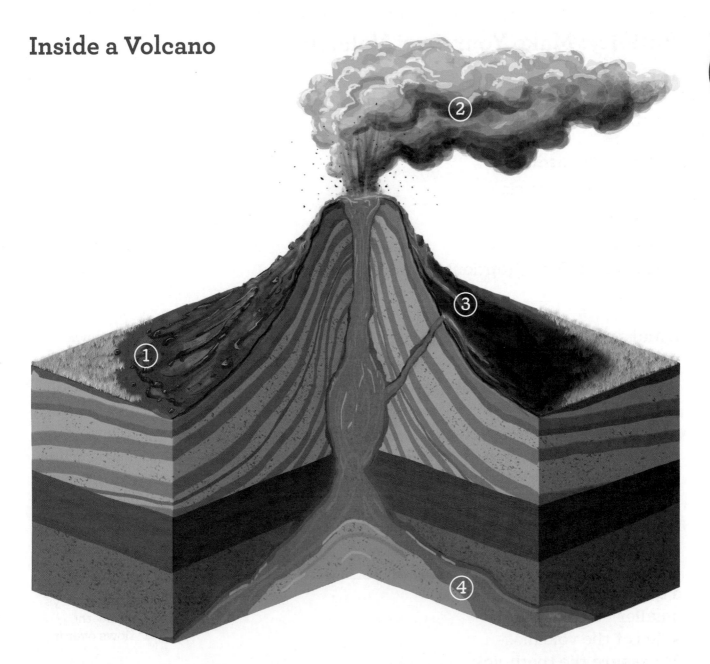

1. Cooling rock: Lava outside the volcano hardens to form new rocks.

2. Gas and ash: When a volcano erupts, lots of gas and crushed rock, called ash, is thrown into the sky.

3. Lava: When magma is pushed out of the volcano and into the cold air, it is called lava.

4. Magma: Deep below a volcano is a mass of magma that is rising upward.

Activity: Make Your Own Volcano

This classic activity makes it easy to see how lava rises up out of a volcano and spills down its sides. But be careful—it's messy.

What you'll need:

- Water-resistant clay
- Baking soda
- Vinegar
- Red food coloring (optional)

1. Make a cone-shaped mound of clay about 4 to 6 inches high, then push your finger into the top of it to make the hole in the volcano. Make the hole as deep as you can!

2. Many volcanoes have smaller vents that also let out lava. You can simulate this by using a toothpick to poke smaller holes in the sides of the volcano. Make sure the toothpick goes all the way through to the big hole at the center.

Note: How much baking soda and vinegar to use will depend on how big your volcano is.

Note: Experiment with volcanoes of different sizes and shapes, or try building a landscape around the volcano with things like canyons and valleys and see how the "lava" flows over it!

3. Put a few spoonfuls of baking soda into the mouth of the volcano. Don't fill your volcano completely, just halfway or so.

4. Have an adult quickly pour some vinegar into the mouth of the volcano, and then watch the lava spew out!

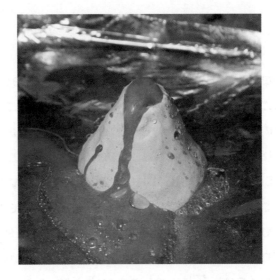

Note: To make it more lava-like, you can put some red food coloring in the vinegar before you pour it in.

This model volcano works because of a chemical reaction between the baking soda and vinegar. While it's not exactly the same as how a volcano works, it still can be a good way to see how lava can flow out of a volcano.

Volcanoes come in different shapes. Tall, cone-shaped volcanoes, like the one you made in this activity, are called **stratovolcanoes**. They are the most famous kind of volcano. They get their name from the strata, or layers, that make up their shape. Every time the volcano erupts, sticky lava hardens

on the outside, making a layer of rock. With more and more eruptions, each new layer of rock builds on top of another, growing into a tall cone. Many stratovolcanoes around the world look like tall, lonely mountains.

Mining

When we need metals like iron or copper, they have to be mined. **Mining** is the process of finding these metals and removing them from the rocks that they formed within. But these metals are not often just waiting there by themselves. They are usually inside certain minerals that contain metals and other elements. Once miners find the right minerals, they can dig them from the ground and process them to get the pure metals out. The place where minerals are taken out of the ground is called a **mine**.

Minerals that are mined for the metals in them are called **ore minerals**, or just **ore**. Most ore minerals are crushed and heated, sometimes with acids and other chemicals, to free the metal from the rest of the mineral.

There are different ways that we can mine minerals. Some mines are giant holes in the ground, some are tunnels into rock, and some are even in rivers.

Modern mining is done by huge pieces of equipment that make it much faster, easier, and safer for the miners.

Many modern mines are enormous pits in the ground where lots of rock is taken out to be processed for valuable metals.

Long ago, mining was done by hand, by breaking into rock with explosives and tools. Many old mines were tunnels that went under mountains. These tunnels are dangerous and could collapse. Mining still happens like this today in some places!

Matching: Ores

Most valuable metals are mined by finding their ore minerals. Many of these metals give their ore minerals certain colors or textures that miners can use to help identify which minerals contain the metals. Below is a list of metals and the colors they often produce in their ore minerals. Use the descriptions to figure out what metals are mined from the ore minerals pictured below.

1. Malachite

2. Psilomelane
(say it "seh-lom-e-lane")

3. Hematite

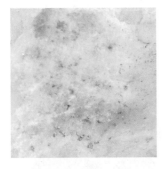

4. Quartz

5. Carnotite

6. Cinnabar

A. Iron ores are often dark brown or black, but they can have a rusty red coloration on their surfaces.

B. Gold is often mined from white quartz that shows tiny bits of yellow metal in it.

C. Uranium ores can be bright vivid yellow in color.

D. Copper ores are often a rich green or blue color.

E. Manganese ores are often black and lumpy.

F. Mercury ores can be deep red or pinkish in color.

Answers on page 119! ☞

Geodes

One of the most interesting kinds of rocks that you can find are called geodes *(say it jee-owd)*. **Geodes** are round rocks shaped like a ball or like an egg, but what's special about them is that they are hollow. And inside them, you may find cool sparkling crystals! Not all geodes have crystals inside, but many do. Minerals like quartz, calcite, pyrite, and many more can be found growing inside a geode.

There are different kinds of geodes around the world, and each formed in a different way. But most formed when a round hole in a rock began to be filled in by minerals. The minerals formed a lining, or shell, around the inside of the hole. Sometimes the minerals filled in the hole completely, but many times they didn't and they remained hollow. Geodes can be found in many types of rock, but most are found in sedimentary rocks, especially limestone.

This is a broken geode full of dirt and clay, and still stuck inside a riverbank where it was found. The mud around it is soft and easy to dig, but the geode itself is hard and tough on the outside.

Geodes look like round balls of rock, but when they're broken open, you'll see that they are hollow and many have cool crystals inside! This one has lots of quartz crystals in it.

This geode is from Algeria and has light-colored amethyst in it.

Where Can I Get a Geode?

Unfortunately, there aren't a large number of places where you can just pick up your own geodes. Some states, like Illinois, Iowa, Missouri, Oregon, and New Mexico, have many places where geodes can be found. But lots of those places are also privately owned, so you'll have to pay to go there. Have an adult help you research where geodes may be found near where you live.

A basket of unbroken geodes for sale

You can also buy geodes from a rock shop or on the internet. Usually they are not expensive, and you may be able to get a whole bag of them for not a lot of money.

Break Open Your Own Geode

Once you've found or purchased your own unbroken geodes, it's time to open them up and see what's inside! Professionals sometimes use specific equipment to split them, but all you'll need is a hammer. Many geodes will break into many little pieces if you just whack them with a hammer, but there are better ways to more carefully open one up. For better success, have an adult help open one up, and make sure you all are wearing safety glasses.

1. If you have a hammer and chisel, use the chisel to carefully tap a groove all the way around the geode without breaking into it yet. Once you've made a complete circle around the geode, go around it with the chisel again, hitting it a little harder at different points in the groove. Eventually, the chisel will break through and the geode should split along the groove you carved (but not always).

Geodes from around the world can have different crystals in them. This geode is from Morocco and has dark amethyst crystals in it.

2. If you don't have a chisel, try putting the geode in an old sock, then tap on it with a hammer. The sock will soften the hammer strikes and will be gentler on the geode if it is a brittle one. The sock will also contain any smaller pieces that break off.

3. Whatever you do, don't just use a hammer to whack it hard! That may work to open the geode, but it will also break it into many pieces and will crush many of the crystals inside.

Agates

Agates *(say it "ag-it")* are a special kind of mineral formation. They are often rounded stones that form inside the spaces or holes inside certain rocks. When whole, they may not look like anything special. But when broken or cut open, you can see that they have amazing ring-like layers inside them! Agates are made up of a special kind of quartz, but they get their different colors from other minerals, like hematite, which can stain the layers. Sometimes the colored layers are in a repeating pattern, like red-white-red-white.

See how this agate's layers have a very clear color pattern that alternates between red, orange, and white?

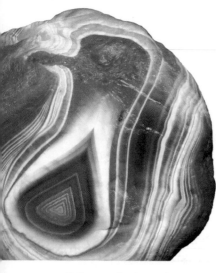

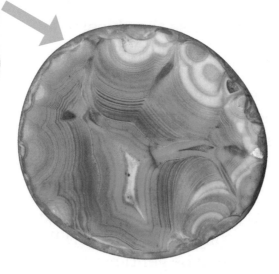

When whole, an agate may look like just a round rock.

But when cut open, the amazing patterns of layers are revealed!

These two orange egg-shaped lumps in this igneous rock are actually whole agates that haven't been broken or cut open.

We know what agates are, but we don't yet know how they formed! They are still a mystery, and scientists are trying to figure out exactly what caused their rings to form. But agates are very hard and tough, and they are often found on beaches or in rivers. They are identified by looking for the layers, which are like rings or circles, but sometimes they are found as little broken pieces that don't have many layers showing.

Agates are found all over the world. This one, from Africa, doesn't have much color, but it does have a perfect pattern.

Agate Layers

The layers in an agate aren't just flat circles or rings. Each layer in an agate is a shell, and each shell contains all the smaller shells within it. But what does that mean?

Have you ever seen nesting dolls? These wooden toys are dolls that open up, and they all fit inside each other. Each doll is a hollow shell that holds all the smaller dolls within it. This is a lot like how an agate's layers work. All the smaller layers fit inside the larger layers, but they are stuck tightly together.

Activity: Make Your Own "Onion Agate"

To better understand how the layers of an agate are shells that fit inside each other, look at an onion!

What you'll need:

- An onion, cut in half
- Food coloring

1. Have an adult help you cut an onion in half to see its layers. Then, carefully pull apart each layer. See how they all have the same shape, but the outer layers are bigger and the inner ones are smaller? This is a lot like the layers in an agate.

2. Once you've separated the layers of an onion, you can use food coloring to dye the edges of alternating layers.

Warning: This will be messy and could stain your hands and clothes!

3. Once you have colored the alternating layers, put the onion back together. Do its layers now look like the layers of an agate?

Rock or Mineral?

When you're out at the beach or walking along a trail and you find a neat stone, you'll want to figure out if it's a rock or a mineral—or maybe even a fossil! Use these tips to start identifying your discoveries:

1. Can you see grains, especially different-colored grains?

Remember that rocks have grains of different minerals in them. So if you think you've found a rock, look for little colored grains. Some rocks, like granite, have lots of large grains that are easy to see. But others have tiny grains that you can only see with magnification. If you found something that doesn't seem to have grains, you may have found a mineral.

2. Does it have little hollow air bubbles?

Some rocks have little round, hollow air bubbles inside them. Minerals won't have bubbles like these. Most rocks with hollow air bubbles are igneous rocks.

3. Is there a lot of it around?

When you find a rock, look around for more—there are often many, many pieces of it around. Minerals are usually a little more rare and you may have to search longer to find another piece. If you find something neat and there's a lot of it around, it's probably a rock.

Rock or Mineral?

4. Is it gritty or dusty to the touch? Does it crumble easily?

If you find something that feels gritty, sandy, or dusty, it's probably a rock. And if it also crumbles and breaks apart easily in your hands, there's a good chance it's a rock. Many times, gritty, crumbly rocks are sedimentary rocks.

5. Does it have lots of layers or stripes of color?

Some things you'll find may have neat layers or stripes of different colors. Layers can be flat and very thin, or they can be wide and wavy, depending on what you've found. Sometimes the layers can even be split apart. If you find something with lots of layers, it's probably a sedimentary or metamorphic rock.

6. Is it glassy or see-through?

If you find something that is shiny like glass, then it's probably a mineral. Most rocks are not glassy. And if you find something that lets some light shine through it, or that you can see through, then it's also probably a mineral.

7. Is it shiny like metal?

If you find something that is shiny like metal, then it's probably a mineral. Most rocks don't have a metallic shine to them.

8. Does it have lots of little edges that all go in the same direction?

Many minerals break apart at certain angles. This means that they don't break irregularly like a piece of glass. Instead, some minerals break in a special way. Like calcite, for example, which usually shows lots of little edges, almost like stair steps, when it's broken. Rocks don't usually break this way.

9. Does it have a particular shape, like pointy spikes or square blocks?

If you find something with a special shape, then it's probably a mineral. If you find things that look like little spikes or cubes, or little barrels or needles, those are probably mineral crystals. Rocks don't form those shapes.

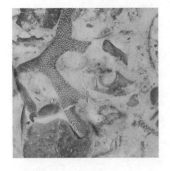

10. Does it have a strange pattern, or look like part of a living thing?

Many of the most common fossils will just look like odd little patterns, textures, or structures inside rocks. If you find something in a rock that looks kind of like little branches or curved shells, or has a pattern that looks a little bit like fabric or honeycomb, then you may have found a fossil.

Speak Like a Geologist

Now that you know so much about what a geologist studies—rocks, minerals, and fossils—you can begin to speak like one! Here is a review of some of the most important terms in a new geologist's vocabulary. Some of them you will recognize from earlier in this book, but a few are new:

Ash: Dust, rock, and fragments of volcanic glass that are blown into the air during some volcanic eruptions.

Bedrock: The top layer of hard rock underneath the soil and other dirt.

Core: The very hot center of the Earth.

Crust: The hard outer layer of the Earth. We live on top of the crust.

Crystal: A solid shape formed when a mineral hardens. Each mineral has a different crystal shape.

Dissolve: When a rock or mineral is absorbed into water or other liquids, disappearing.

Druse *("drooz")*: A crust of mineral crystals that form on the inside of a hollow space.

Eruption *("ee-rup-shun")*: When a volcano throws lava, gas, and ash onto the Earth's surface and into the air.

Extinct: When all the animals of a particular type die out and disappear from the Earth, like the dinosaurs.

Quiz Time

1. Look at the geodes on page 108. See how little crystals line the inside of the geodes? What is that?

_____

2. When looking at rock strata and you find one layer underneath another, what does that tell you about the lower layer?

_____

3. What layer of the Earth is below the crust and above the core?

_____

Answers on page 119! ☞

Fossil: The remains of ancient plants and animals that turned into minerals and are preserved in rocks

Grain Size: The size of the little mineral particles that make up rocks.

Hardness: How hard it is to scratch a mineral.

Igneous Rock *("ig-nee-us")*: Rocks that form when molten rock cools off and hardens; this can happen deep in the Earth or on the Earth's surface.

Lava *("lah-vah")*: Melted rocks that have been pushed onto the Earth's surface.

Luster *("luss-terr")*: How shiny a mineral is.

Magma *("mayg-ma")*: Melted rocks that are still deep underground.

Mantle: The hot layer inside the Earth that is just below the crust. It is so hot that rocks can melt.

Massive: A mineral that formed as a mass of tightly compact crystals or grains instead of as a well-formed single crystal. Massive minerals appear in irregular masses.

Metamorphic Rock *("meh-tuh-mor-fik")*: Rocks that form when older rocks are heated up and pressed by lots of weight; this changes the old rocks into new types.

Mineral *("min-er-ul")*: A material that forms when a special kind of chemical hardens. Minerals form as crystals inside rocks.

Quiz Time

1. What are the big moving pieces of the Earth's crust called?

_____

2. If you dig a deep hole in the dirt and at the bottom you hit hard, solid rock, what is that rock called?

_____

3. What is the name for magma that has been pushed up and out of the Earth?

_____

Answers on page 119! ☞

Speak Like a Geologist

Mining: The process of removing valuable materials, such as metals, from the Earth.

Ore Mineral *("or")*: A mineral that we mine for the useful metals it contains.

Precipitation: When minerals that are dissolved in water begin to clump together and crystallize due to a change in the water, such as when it cools down.

Rock: A group of minerals that formed together in a tight mass. Rocks can form inside the Earth or on the Earth's surface.

Rock Strata *("stra-tuh")*: The different layers of rocks that make up the Earth's crust; the oldest are at the bottom and the youngest are at the top.

Sediment: Little particles of rocks, minerals, and even plants and animals that have been worn down by weathering. Sediments are things like sand and clay.

Sedimentary Rock *("sed-i-ment-air-y")*: Rocks that form when sediments stick together and harden. This usually happens in or near water.

Stratovolcano *("stra-tow-vol-cane-oh")*: Tall, cone-shaped volcanoes that are made up of layers, or strata, of hardened lava from each eruption.

Tectonic Plates *("tek-ton-ic")*: The large sheets of rock that make up the Earth's crust. They float on top of the mantle and move around slowly, bumping into each other and causing earthquakes and volcanoes.

Vesicle *("veh-sih-kuhl")*: Round bubbles of gas that were trapped inside igneous rocks when they cooled.

Volcano: An opening, or vent, in the ground where molten rock and gas is forced upward onto the Earth's surface.

Weathering: When water, wind, ice, and plants break and wear down rocks and minerals.

Quiz Answers

Page 9: 1. Rock 2. Crystal 3. Rock 4. Crystal 5. Fossil 6. Fossil

Page 11: 1. Crust 2. Upper Mantle 3. Lower Mantle
4. Outer Core 5. Inner Core

Page 16: 1. Permian 2. Bacteria

Page 19: 1. About 530 million years ago 2. Carboniferous 3. Amphibians

Page 20: 1. Triassic 2. They grew to large sizes/got bigger

Page 23: 1. Birds 2. Triassic, Jurassic, and Cretaceous 3. No

Page 25: 1. The bottommost one 2. No 3. The *Triceratops* fossil

Pages 30–31: 1. B 2. C 3. A 4. A 5. A and C 6. C

Page 33: 1. F 2. H 3. C 4. B 5. D 6. A 7. E 8. G

Page 35: 1. E 2. A 3. B 4. C 5. D 6. F

Page 41: 1. Amethyst 2. Smoky Quartz 3. Rose Quartz 4. Citrine
5. Morion Quartz

Page 43: 1. F 2. D 3. B 4. C 5. E 6. A

Page 55: 1. Semiprecious 2. Precious 3. Precious 4. Nonprecious
5. Semiprecious 6. Nonprecious 7. Precious 8. Semiprecious

Page 60: A. 1 B. 4 C. 3 D. 2

Page 71: 1. Sedimentary 2. Igneous 3. Mica

Page 72: 1. Sedimentary 2. Sedimentary 3. Metamorphic 4. Metamorphic
5. Igneous 6. Igneous 7. Igneous 8. Sedimentary 9. Metamorphic

Page 75: 1. It would need to melt deep in the Earth, then cool and harden
2. It would have to metamorphose first (which would happen before it
was ever deep enough to melt) 3. Metamorphic 4. Igneous 5. All of them

Page 85: 1. Fossilization 2. Sedimentary 3. Minerals

Page 87: 1. They went extinct 2. They lived in water/oceans

Page 89: 1. F 2. D 3. E 4. G

Page 100: 1. Sinkhole 2. Plateaus and buttes 3. Acid

Page 107: 1. D 2. E 3. A 4. B 5. C 6. F

Page 116: 1. Druse 2. It's older 3. Mantle

Page 117: 1. Tectonic plates 2. Bedrock 3. Lava

Geology Bingo

Test your geology knowledge with a game of Bingo!

Have an adult help you cut out the following four pages so that you and your friends can go on a Bingo hunt for rocks, minerals, and landforms. Here's how it works:

Look for the rocks, minerals, or landforms noted in each square. When you find one, cross out the square with an X or color it in. Keep searching for the things in the squares until you've made a row, column, or diagonal line of 5 connected squares.

Take note that the center square is a free space! Everyone gets that square.

B I N G O

Rock that has been rounded by water	Sand	White rock or mineral	Rock or mineral that lets light shine through it	Rock with speckled mineral grains, like granite
Building or walkway made of stone	Tall landform *(hint: look for a mountain, cliff, or big hill)*	Gravel	Metal that has been mined *(hint: look for something made of iron)*	Igneous rock
Sedimentary rock	Rock with a hole in it	**FREE SPACE**	Rock with layers or stripes	Crumbly rock or mineral that falls apart easily
Huge rock (one too big to lift!)	Shiny rock or mineral	Metamorphic rock	Landform made by weathering *(hint: look for a river or valley)*	Mineral or rock so soft that your fingernail will scratch it
Mineral or rock that can be scratched with a coin	Black rock or mineral	Mineral or rock that will leave a mark on other rocks, like chalk	Silt or clay (very fine sediment)	Red or orange rock or mineral

Journal Entry #1

An important part of geology is recording where a rock or mineral was found. All good geologists take careful notes! Next time you find a cool rock, mineral, or fossil, use this space to write down exactly where you found it. This information is very important for scientific study.

_____

_____

_____

_____

_____

_____

_____

_____

_____

_____

_____

B I N G O

Mineral or rock that will leave a mark on other rocks, like chalk	Igneous Rock	Black rock or mineral	Rock or mineral that lets light shine through it	Tall landform *(hint: look for a mountain, cliff, or big hill)*
Building or walkway made of stone	Rock with speckled mineral grains, like granite	Gravel	Igneous rock	White rock or mineral
Metamorphic rock	Rock with layers or stripes	FREE SPACE	Rock with a hole in it	Mineral or rock that can be scratched with a coin
Huge rock (one too big to lift!)	Landform made by weathering *(hint: look for a river or valley)*	Sedimentary rock	Shiny rock or mineral	Mineral or rock so soft that your fingernail will scratch it
Metal that has been mined *(hint: look for something made of iron)*	Rock that has been rounded by water	Sand	Red or orange rock or mineral	Silt or clay (very fine sediment)

Journal Entry #2

An important part of geology is recording where a rock or mineral was found. All good geologists take careful notes! Next time you find a cool rock, mineral, or fossil, use this space to write down exactly where you found it. This information is very important for scientific study.

_____

_____

_____

_____

_____

_____

_____

_____

_____

_____

_____

B I N G O

Crumbly rock or mineral that falls apart easily	Sand	Rock or mineral that lets light shine through it	White rock or mineral	Metamorphic rock
Igneous rock	Tall landform *(hint: look for a mountain, cliff, or big hill)*	Red or orange rock or mineral	Metal that has been mined *(hint: look for something made of iron)*	Mineral or rock that can be scratched with a coin
Landform made by weathering *(hint: look for a river or valley)*	Rock that has been rounded by water	FREE SPACE	Rock with layers or stripes	Mineral or rock that will leave a mark on other rocks, like chalk
Huge rock (one too big to lift!)	Mineral or rock so soft that your fingernail will scratch it	Rock with speckled mineral grains, like granite	Sedimentary rock	Shiny rock or mineral
Building or walkway made of stone	Black rock or mineral	Rock with a hole in it	Silt or clay (very fine sediment)	Gravel

Journal Entry #3

An important part of geology is recording where a rock or mineral was found. All good geologists take careful notes! Next time you find a cool rock, mineral, or fossil, use this space to write down exactly where you found it. This information is very important for scientific study.

_____

_____

_____

_____

_____

_____

_____

_____

_____

_____

BINGO

Metamorphic rock	Sedimentary rock	White rock or mineral	Gravel	Mineral or rock that can be scratched with a coin
Tall landform *(hint: look for a mountain, cliff, or big hill)*	Building or walkway made of stone	Landform made by weathering *(hint: look for a river or valley)*	Metal that has been mined *(hint: look for something made of iron)*	Rock with speckled mineral grains, like granite
Crumbly rock or mineral that falls apart easily	Rock with a hole in it	FREE SPACE	Rock with layers or stripes	Sand
Mineral or rock that will leave a mark on other rocks, like chalk	Shiny rock or mineral	Mineral or rock so soft that your fingernail will scratch it	Rock or mineral that lets light shine through it	Red or orange rock or mineral
Igneous rock	Black rock or mineral	Huge rock (one too big to lift!)	Silt or clay (very fine sediment)	Rock that has been rounded by water

Journal Entry #4

An important part of geology is recording where a rock or mineral was found. All good geologists take careful notes! Next time you find a cool rock, mineral, or fossil, use this space to write down exactly where you found it. This information is very important for scientific study.

_____

_____

_____

_____

_____

_____

_____

_____

_____

_____

Recommended Reading

Bates, Robert L., editor. *Dictionary of Geological Terms, 3rd Edition.* New York: Anchor Books, 1984.

Bonewitz, Ronald Louis. *Smithsonian Rock and Gem.* New York: DK Publishing, 2005.

Chesteman, Charles W. *The Audubon Society Field Guide to North American Rocks and Minerals.* New York: Knopf, 1979.

Dorling Kindersley (DK). *The Rock and Gem Book: And other Treasures of the Natural World.* London: DK Publishing, 2016.

Johnsen, Ole. *Minerals of the World.* New Jersey: Princeton University Press, 2004.

Lynch, Dan R. *Fossils for Kids.* Cambridge, Minnesota: Adventure Publications, 2020.

Lynch, Dan R. *Rock Collecting for Kids.* Cambridge, Minnesota: Adventure Publications, 2018.

Mottana, Annibale, et al. *Simon and Schuster's Guide to Rocks and Minerals.* New York: Simon and Schuster, 1978.

Pellant, Chris. *Rocks and Minerals.* New York: Dorling Kindersley Publishing, 2002.

Pough, Frederick H. *Rocks and Minerals.* Boston: Houghton Mifflin, 1988.

Robinson, George W. *Minerals.* New York: Simon & Schuster, 1994.

Tomecek, Steve. *National Geographic Kids: Everything Rocks and Minerals.* National Geographic, 2011.

Photo Credits

Cover Illustrations by **Fallon Venable**

All images copyright by **Dan R. Lynch** unless otherwise noted.
Dr. Julie A. Kirsch: 130 (author photo); **Fallon Venable:** 1, 3, 5, 120, 121, 123, 125, 127, 129, and 130 (background illustrations).

The following image is licensed according to a Attribution 4.0 International (CC BY 4.0) license, available here: https://creativecommons.org/licenses/by/4.0/
"Elaborate plumage patterning in a Cretaceous bird" in *Peerj* by Quanguo Li, Julia A. Clarke, Ke-Qin Gao, Jennifer A. Peteya, and Matthew D. Shawkey; original image available here: DOI: 0.7717/peerj.5831

Images used under license from Shutterstock:
Adrian Baker: 105 (bottom); **Akiyoko:** 38 (hand); **Albert Russ:** 6 (top), 32 (2nd), 33 (3 & 6), 35 (2 & 4), 38 (fluorite), 39 (corundum & topaz), 40 (aquamarine, bixbite, emerald, gray beryl), 41 (1, 4 & 5), 49 (hematite, right), 52 (fluorite, right & tourmaline, right), 53 (chalcopyrite, right), 54 (ruby crystals), 55 (3 & 7), 107 (6), 111 (top), 114 (middle left); **Alejandro Lafuente Lopez:** 33 (2), 38 (calcite), 52 (malachite, right), 39 (orthoclase feldspar); **Aleksandr Pobedimskiy:** 62 (bottom right), 64 (bottom left), 72 (1), 78 (limestone, left), 91 (bottom right); **Alexlky:** 14 (bottom right); **Alexxxey:** 28 (bottom right); **Almarina:** 54 (diamond); **Amanda Mohler:** 29 (bottom right); **Anastasia Bulanova:** 38 (talc), 53 (talc, right); **Andrei Nekrassov:** 17 (top left); **Andrew Mayovskyy:** 30 (1B); **Andriy Kananovych:** 49 (geothite, right), 72 (2); **Anmbph:** 29 (middle left), 92 (bottom left); **anne-tipodees:** 40 (bottom right); **Anton Dangov:** 23 (bottom left); **Arjen de Ruiter:** 87 (right); **Artem Gorlanov:** 30 (3B); **Atstock Productions:** 31 (6B); **Avkost:** 61 (pumice); **B. K. Tshimanga:** 64 (top right); **Barks:** 85 (bottom); **Belyak Olga:** 67 (bottom left); **Beth Ruggiero-York:** 30 (2C); **Bjoern Wylezich:** 8 (4th), 39 (quartz), 48 (quartz, left), 52 (epidote, right), 55 (5), 89 (A), 108 (bottom right), 109 (bottom); **Bjul:** 27 (top left); **Bleung:** 18 (bottom left); **Bon Appetit:** 92 (top left); **Branko Jovanovic:** 50 (pyroxene, right); **Breck P. Kent:** 72 (4), 86 (bottom right), 89 (F), 94 (right); **Bruce MacQueen:** 89 (4); **BW Folsom:** 86 (top right); **Captain Wang:** 6-7 (bottom); **Carlosdelacalle:** 49 (pyrite, right); **Catmando:** 22 (bottom right); **Chakapong:** 30 (2B); **Checubus:** 26 (right); **Chris Cornish:** 72 (8); **ChWeiss:** 50 (Mica, left); **Cjansuebsri:** 18 (bottom right); **Cloete55:** 57 (middle left); **COULANGES:** 51 (garnet, right); **CreativeFireStock:** 41 (3); **Dafinchi:** 41 (2); **Daniel Eskridge:** 21 (bottom left); **Darkydoors:** 27 (bottom left); **Dave Alle Photography:** 30 (3A); **Deni Sugandi:** 29 (top right), 102 (left); **Denis_Belitsky:** 30 (1A); **Dewin ID:** 19 (top); **Elena Larina:** 57 (bottom right); **Eleonimages:** 91 (middle right); **Eric Isselee:** 89 (3); **Eric Valenne geostory:** 31 (5C); **ExpediTom:** 27 (top right); **Fokin Oleg:** 77 (conglomerate, right); **Francisco Sandoval Guate:** 3 (5B); **Frank Bach:** 14 (middle right); **Gartland:** 90 (left); **goran_safarek:** 30 (1C); **gunungkawi:** 56 (top); **Heller Joachim:** 66 (right); **Henri Koskinen:** 33 (4), 43 (4); **Herschel Hoffmeyer:** 21 (top right & bottom right), 22 (bottom left, both); **Iamnong:** 29 (top left); **IM_photo:** 31 (4C), 99 (top); **Imagine Earth Photography:** 66 (left); **Iosmandarinas:** 59 (bottom); **Issarawat Tattong:** 88 (shrimp, right); **itakefotos4u:** 63 (middle left); **Jeff Holcombe:** 32 (4th); **Jennifer Mellon Photos:** 18 (shark, top right); **Jiri Hera:** 32 (3rd); **Jirik V:** 43 (6), 55 (1); **JJ Mad-**

About the Author

Dan R. Lynch grew up in his parents' rock shop, learning to identify rocks and minerals from a young age. Always an artist and writer, he combined his graphic design degree with his background in rocks to write more than 20 books about rocks and minerals. With his books, he strives to help novices "decode" the complex terms and concepts in geology by writing in an easy-to-understand way and approaching every topic with a "from the ground up" approach.

He has always been fascinated by the natural world and all of its little details that most people don't pay any attention to, and he hopes his books can spark curiosity in his readers young and old. Dan currently lives in Madison, Wisconsin, with his wife, Julie, and their cat, Daisy.

Crystallized magnetite— a favorite of the author